THE LIVES OF
CARL ATMAN

∞

A Love Story by
MORRIS W. WALKER

Published by microEPIC Productions
Cover Design: Skye Walker
www.microepic.com
1.541.602.8703

Dedication

I claim to be a writer, but in attempting to describe
how I feel about my family relative to this novel
and life in general, I find myself at a loss for words;
gratitude for love, compassion, companionship,
inspiration, faith and support and non-stop
encouragement just don't seem to be enough.

I owe them everything.

Thank you Lynn, Amoris and Skye,
this book is totally dedicated to you

Many Thanks

Sally for all her assistance in the
process and her Aloha spirit

Everett Peacock, for being an
inspirational writer and cheerleader

Valentino Cano for early proofing

Dave, Bodil and Kula for
being part of our Maui Ohana

Marsha and Lesley for being
my ever-positive sisters

Deidre Reigel for introducing me to Judith

Judith Hemphill for amazing editing, enthusiasm
and many good times on the phone

Jim Barnhart for sharing his ever positive energy

And to the Atman in all of us

Introduction

Time. I've always liked the way that word stands on its own, the way it resonates in English, the visions it invokes in a reader's mind. I'm quite sure it has similar effects in other languages: spoken, sung or signed. It speaks of vast distances we can never comprehend in one lifetime, defines our beginning and end, and therefore establishes that it is indeed our most valued gift, second only to...
Love.

Our human lifespans seem designed to enable us to experience the richness, and consequences of this greatest of all gifts with a few fortunate souls we meet along our wandering way.

But, what if we could extend that experience farther? Across many lifetimes, across time? Imagine the depths of emotion that might be waiting for our souls to swim through? Imagine, even if only for a fictional moment, that this could all be done with a continuity that allowed for the accumulation of a grand perspective, one normally reserved for the gods?

Some religions speak of how humans were created in God's image, what if they're right? What if the ancients understood, far better than we do today, the ramifications of that reflection - the responsibilities?

You can ask Carl Atman about that, once you meet him in this engaging work by my dear friend Morris Walker. This story puts a beautiful texture to the concepts of time, of love and to continuity that I found quite fascinating. I suspect all that quality time Morris has spent on the island of Maui has enlightened the process of translating what the lucky ones understand implicitly into what you, the lucky reader, will soon find.

Enjoy within the quiet confines of your imagination.

Aloha

Everett Peacock
Kula, Maui, Hawaii
March 2013

Preface

Each soul's journey through life on planet earth is an ultimate adventure.

The greater picture of the billions of lives and these stories are a cosmic phenomenon we can never comprehend in this life. But along with our God-given intuition and creative power, we can imagine. And in all our lives, we learn at one point or another that there is inner guidance available for us if we merely tune in.

I told someone that I had written a book about reincarnation. She asked, "Is it fiction?"

And the only answer I could find for her was, "That's a good question."

I have written books, short stories, essays, articles, songs, poems and countless scripts and comedy routines. The Lives of Carl Atman is a book that I have been wanting to write for years, maybe for lifetimes. I was inspired by the observable cycles of life that ebb and flow all around us throughout our lives and I felt compelled to write this story.

My hope above all else, is that you enjoy the journey.

Table of Contents

Chapter One

Kimo

Alaxsxaq
(Later named Alaska)
1532 AD

The Inuit woman Quannik held Kimo's arm. He was the most powerful of those who were known as the first people. His tribal name was Taliriktug, which meant *strong arm* by the Eskimos of Siku. Quannik and Kimo were "One," as the Eskimo tribe called a man and woman together. There were 80 people in their village, located to the west near the big water that did not freeze.

Neither the blackness nor bitter cold outside their igloo stopped them from watching the spectacular lights of the Aurora Borealis, what the white people would eventually call the Northern lights.

Eskimos had arrived in Alaxsxaq from coastal Siberia thousands of years before Quannik and Kimo became first people. They spoke the Yupik language similar to Eskimos in Siberia.

Life in the vast frozen tundra of the ancient Northwest was very hard. But the incredibly rugged Eskimos had known nothing but frozen hardships since their ancestors' ancestors.

Kimo was the largest and most agile of the men; because of his natural intuitive insight and alacrity, he was also the greatest hunter of them all. He somehow knew when the seals would surface from an uglu (seal hole in the ice), and he was lightning fast spearing them and dragging them out.

Like many Inuit wolf hunters, he would coat his razor sharp knife with blood from another animal and let it freeze and then coat it again and again until eventually it was thick with frozen blood. He would then secure the handle firmly in the ice with the blade up. When an ulva (wolf) would smell the bloody blade, he would begin to lick it, slicing his tongue and never knowing it. He would voraciously continue to lick the sharp blade over and over until his tongue was bloody ribbons, unaware of drinking his own blood. He would quickly bleed to death.

It seemed a cruel way to watch a mighty animal die, even though it was a common practice. Kimo honored the great wolf and prayed for its soul. As opposed to other animals he hunted, he had visions of a wolf that was his friend and hero in some distant warm time and place. Therefore, he cried each time he took the life of a wolf, and he finally decided that this mighty wolf was the last one he would hunt. Quannik would make coats and gloves and muck-lucks for Kimo and herself from other animals, but from that moment on, he would never hunt ulva the wolf again. When Quannik asked why, he teared up a little and said adamantly, "I know now that the wolf is my friend, and someday I will have a mighty dog like a wolf!"

She smiled a knowing smile and nodded. She wanted to say, *"Not in this life,"* but she didn't, although her premonition was quite right. It was carved in the ice that would never melt. A fact.

Kimo provided the food and protection for his woman, and she maintained the igloo, prepared the meals, and kept their surroundings in order. Winters were long and brutal, but it was all they knew. They loved each other and their lives together.

When Kimo would return after hours or days in the wild, his loving Quannik would help him remove his heavy bearskin coat, lay him on his back, and remove his wolf skin boots. Then she would pull his padded socks off. Pulling her top up, she would kneel at his feet, revealing her large full breasts. Moaning loudly and happily, he would lift his tired legs and let her cuddle and warm his feet on her chest. She smiled a huge, adoring smile as he responded with a deep, happy sigh. They were in love. Love made their frozen domain warm in addition to the fire they kept burning with dried animal dung.

Quannik (which meant snowflake) and Kimo were spiritual people and often prayed to their god, Agloolik. Agloolik was the good spirit that lived under the ice and helped Kimo with hunting and fishing.

There were other gods, but Agloolik was the god they loved the most, and with belief in him they knew they would always have deer and whale blubber and huge trout and other fish.

Kimo had visions. He told only Quannik about his dreams. The other first people would call him mad.

But in the summers when the sun was so warm on his face, he would come home and tell Quannik that he believed that there were other lands on the edge of the big water that never froze, lands that did not have ice. He said that such lands had sand like the summer sand near the water, only it was black. Quannik would wince at the thought of sand being black. Kimo, would comfort her and explain that in such a place they could be naked outdoors and never cold, surrounded by tall, skinny trees with ferns at the top and large edible nuts.

Life was hard on the first people, and Quannik knew Kimo's visions were dreams that could only happen in another world. But she would humor him and say, "Where would Agloolik live, if there was no ice?"

"Just under the water, Snowflake, just under the water." Quannik would smile but believed not that such things existed. How could seals live, or the shesh (brown bears) without ice and snow? But she loved sharing his visions. It made him happy. And when he was happy, he wanted to "laugh" with Quannik. This meant make love. And so they did . . . a lot. They had no children yet, but they wanted to and didn't know that Quannik was with child and had been for a month.

Kimo explained to Quannik that at night he dreamt that they were in a wonderfully hot land, like some days in the arctic summer but without the giant mosquitoes. This was not the place with the black sand, but a brown dirt land that was warm with rocky hills and shacks. Once again, she loved the dreams and humored him, wanting to believe.

Kimo spent many hours in his kayak fishing with his friend Torngasak over the years. One overcast day when hiking back as they were looking out for more game, especially tucktu (deer), Torngasak was the first one to see a young buck as they walked from behind a snow bank. Kimo was silent and swift as he set down his pack and pulled out his spear. The throw was rapid and accurate. The small buck fell quickly when the spear penetrated his chest. The men bent over the body and thanked the gods for his life.

Torngasak picked up the backpacks, spears, fish and fishing gear. Kimo was one of few men who could actually pick up a 125 pound buck, throw it over his broad shoulders and carry it for two miles in snow sometimes knee deep. And so he did.

When Quannik saw the magnificent buck along with the line of fish Torngasak tossed on the snow covered ground, she was delighted.

She knelt down with a skinning knife and, smiling up at Kimo first, she then inserted the knife in the buck's stomach to begin gutting the animal. The deer suddenly came to life, and spasmodically flung its body over. Quannik began to stand up and the animal's hoof hit her squarely in the left eye . . .

Kimo immediately grabbed the buck's front legs and, swinging it in a circle, threw it six feet away. It made an agonized sound as its neck snapped, and it landed on the ground, dead.

Quickly dropping to Quannik's side, Kimo could see the horrible gauge the hoof had left where her eye used to be. Blood was pouring out of the opening.

Torngasak had already begun sprinting to Desna's igloo. Desna meant the boss or healer; he was an old and wise man, who knew more about injuries and healing than anyone.

He quickly returned with Torngasak. He was able to stop the bleeding with rags his wife Anyu (which meant angel) had brought with them.

Desna talked to Kimo as he sat cross-legged and watched Anyu caring for Quannik.

"You are brave and strong, Kimo, and your most beautiful wife, Snowflake, will be all right, but you must pray to the gods and spend time in silence beside her while she heals. But Kimo, my son, Akkikitok (the evil god of the sea) has done this as is his way. Now you must be strong and always see Quannik as she has always been. Her eye is gone and there will be a scar. But her heart is pure."

"Desna," said Kimo. "Nothing could make me see Quannik as anything but lovely. I just want her to live, and for us to have a son and be able to watch the great lights together in the coming years. She will still have one eye to see the sky lights and the light in the eye of her son. Desna, you know about these things, will Quannik have our baby?"

Desna looked at Anyu, who had her hand on Quannik's stomach at the time, and had heard the conversation. Anyu nodded affirmatively. Desna turned to Kimo and said, "Quannik is with child now."

Kimo smiled and scooted over beside Quannik, taking her hand and leaning down to put his nose touching hers. He peered deeply into her big, inquisitive almond eye and told her the news. She smiled.

"You will be fine, my sweet Snowflake. There are many years ahead for us."

And so there were. Kimo Chu (Beaver) was a fat baby. Quannik's left eye area healed over, but could never open again.

Kimo Chu followed in his father's footsteps and became the greatest hunter of the tribe.

Kimo and Quannik never stopped dreaming of warm places and eating summer vegetables in a warm land year round. When Quannik died, Kimo followed a few days later. He was fifty-two years old, older than his beloved Quannik, which was very old considering the unimaginable hardship of life of an Eskimo in those ancient times.

Young Kimo Chu took each one of them in the family kayak out to sea to be left in the water with the ancestors. He prayed to the good god of the sea,

Agloolik, who had always been good to his family, to keep them warm always with many fish and summer vegetables. And let them find the world with the black sand, long, tall, curved trees, year round warm weather, and lights in the day time like the great night lights of the Eskimo planet. Kimo had told Kimo Chu many times of his visions.

Though Quannik could never comprehend such a place, Kimo Chu believed his father's vision and knew that Agloolik could make it happen for a good man like his father, the one the people called Kimo, the great.

Chapter Two

Shankara

India

The British East Indies Company was founded in 1599 by a group of merchants in search of nothing more than "quiet trade." However, circumstances thwarted these peaceful intentions, and the results were that for over 250 years the British would find themselves more and more in the role of conquerors and governors rather than traders.

Once India was indeed "conquered," many around the world were exposed to the British cliché that stated that India was "the crown jewel of the British Empire." The humiliated Indians suffered the abuse of the "conquering nation of Britain" for what seemed like forever, until Mahatma Gandhi and his supporters overthrew the British government peacefully, and freedom from tyranny finally came to India in 1948.

Gandhi did this by using non-violence, even though the British were brutally cruel to many Indians. Since the British were there for profits, Gandhi decided that if the people didn't buy anything from them, then the invaders would have no reason to be there. Gandhi helped establish India's new government, and his helping overthrow British rule eventually led to India's independence.

India became the largest Democracy in the world and set a worldwide precedence for the ultimate power of peace, from a country steeped in the ancient traditions of peace and love through prayer and meditation.

After The British East Indies Company was founded, Shankara Vishnu was born in 1651. His family was of a lower caste in a village outside of Calcutta. His was a spiritual family that practiced ancient Hindu traditions of meditation for God realization, with the ultimate goal of reaching a state of Yoga known as Raja Yoga. They were strict vegetarians, as their ancestors had been. It was also, therefore, their belief not to kill animals of any kind.

Shankara's father was a sandal maker, and his older brother, Seshu, was learning the trade. Shankara was only twelve; he loved his name as it meant "the great one." His father and mother felt he was destined to become a Guru in the Swami order, a realized Master in meditation and transmutation into cosmic consciousness. Shankara did have the feeling that perhaps being a Guru might be his destiny in some lifetime. Yet he felt his most powerful potential would not be in just meditating in this life, but as a great warrior. His own vision was that someday he would be part of a Gurkha regiment and that he would be revered as a conquering colonel or general, wielding his khukuri (curving Nepalese knife) in a brigade of Gurkhas. He felt he would be a perfect fit in that manifestation. Shankara had heard that if a man said he was not afraid of dying, he was either lying or he was a Gurkha. He liked that. True bravery. He had fashioned a khukuri out of a piece of local rosewood, which almost resembled the form of a real Gurkha sword naturally. His brother helped him finish it, but Seshu made him promise not to tell either his mother or his father that he had been involved.

Shankara loved his papa, Babu, and his mother, Maji. But he absolutely adored Megah, his 90-year-old grandfather. Megah loved Shankara, as well, and they shared many precious moments. Shankara could tell Megah anything and know that it would be kept secret. So he shared his dreams and visions of being a soldier that he could not share with his parents, or even his brother, only with Megah.

Megah was ancient and kind. In just a few words, he let Shankara know that the greatest battle in life was with oneself, with his own ego. Shankara listened, but dreamt of being a Gurkha simultaneously.

"Youth is passionate," Megah thought to himself, "a common ego trait with the young." But with age, he knew, the passion would change to women and then maybe self-realization; only time would tell.

Because of the uncommonly close bond between Megah and the boy, Shankara had decided that to live a righteous life and become as old as Megah would be a good thing, even though Megah was very wrinkled and dark because of his natural skin color and countless years under the sizzling Indian sun. Shankara held him in high esteem.

Megah would also instruct Shankara to focus on the third eye, known as the Kutastha Chaitanya, the space between the eyebrows. Megah's advice to Shankara fell on welcome ears, and Shankara felt that if he could be wise as well, it was acceptable to him to be an old man like Megah someday, honored and respected by one and all.

Periodically, Maji gently instructed Shankara in meditation, ancient chants, and ceremonies in a clearing not far from the village near the large rock hills. She would lovingly sit with him for a while, chanting and teaching simple meditation techniques. Shankara adored the chants and knew somehow that music would always be with him, whether it was devotional music or just social music. He especially loved playing the Indian drum known as the tabla. Maji knew that Shankara's greatest teacher was Megah, almost like a Guru, and that was fine; he was her father and admired by all as a spiritual teacher. While Maji was meditating with Shankara, she would open her eyes and see the form of her boy in deep meditation, perfectly still, and then she would quietly steal away home to prepare a dinner, sometimes of dahl and rice, as a reward for his devotion and dedication.

Little did she know that he would peek, too, and as soon as she was gone, he would sneak over to a nearby tree and pull out his Khukuri sword and a stuffed doll that he had found in an alley. Then, like a mighty Gurkha general, he would imagine stories and act them out. He would set the ragged doll, wrapped in an old burlap type of bag, by a tree stump in the bushes and then reenact his favorite imaginary story. It was a vision of himself riding a magnificent horse in full regalia in the midst of a battle, suddenly seeing a helpless child deserted in the forest. He could see himself dismounting, throwing his leg over the saddle as his steed came to a stop, and he would leap off, landing firmly on both feet, brandishing his knife like a seasoned circus performer.

As he reached the child, three British assailants would attack him. Swirling like a Turkish dervish, he would quickly dispatch the first two and be in full battle with the third, when something would cause him to stop dreaming and playing out his silly story. He felt a kind of guilt; his shoulders slumped, and he looked in all directions to make sure no one saw him as he carefully hid his sword and the baby doll he was willing to die for. It was a stupid game he played, he thought, to battle for a child. He didn't even like babies. And he would never be a Gurkha.

Maji wanted him to go to an Ashram and be taught by monks of the swami order to meditate. Therefore, he would sit cross-legged in the traditional fashion of meditation and try very hard to focus on the lessons Maji and Megah were always reiterating. He thought about what she said about God being within. There were many Hindu gods, and he could never understand what she meant when she would say God is inside you. "Divine Mother is part of you, Shankara." In India quite often God is referred to as Divine Mother.

Always his fleeting dreams of battle would fade. But as his little body calmed down, and he began to be more relaxed, there was still no way he could get the battle of Shankara completely out of his head. He even had one dream over and over of the same battle in a faraway land on a magnificent strange stallion, with the enemy all dressed in grey uniforms and a live child to be rescued. He was a full grown man with a red beard, which made him laugh. He'd never known anyone with a red beard. That's why he thought it was in a different land, or just in his vivid imagination.

One day while strolling back from his meditation and his dream battle, he ran into his favorite friend from school.

"Namaste, Maya," said Shankara.

"Namaste, Shankara," she said. (The traditional greeting *Namaste* actually means, "The God in me bows to the God in you.")

She was a small, quiet girl named Maya (which means illusion), a petite ten-year-old, two years younger than he. She was indeed a beautiful child, with dark skin, a clef chin and deep dimples when she smiled, but shunned by many because she was born with her left eyelid locked shut. No one knew why it was sealed with no trace of a lash or an opening. So the children made fun of her, and parents told their children that there must be some sort of curse and to avoid her. There was an unreasonable social stigma about the deformed eye. To Shankara, however, she was the loveliest girl on the planet. Her right eye was big and bright; in fact, the ebony pupil glistened with excitement when she saw Shankara. But to others, she was very reserved and withdrawn.

They really brought the best out in each other and spent as much time together as they could.

Shankara didn't always call her Maya. He just called her "M," and she liked that. She called him Shankara, and liked it because she knew it meant "the great one," and to her he was just that. Sometimes she would call him "Shankara, the great." He had told her about his dream of being a Gurhka colonel or general, but he had never told her about his sword or the doll he rescued in playing out his fantasy. He wanted to take her into his vision and show her how he could fight, but he felt he couldn't do that until he actually finished the battle in his mind some day.

Maya's parents, like Shankara's, instructed her in devotion and meditation to Bhagavan Krishna, the most popular of all Hindu gods. But Maya also had other visions, like Shankara, of focusing her life on being a mother, and because of Shankara, she envisioned her adult life with a soldier just like Shankara.

They often talked about Sri Krishna, but also other gods, like Buddha and a mysterious saint called Jesus, the Christ, from somewhere else in the world. They both felt an unusual kinship they didn't understand with this prophet named Jesus, but they never talked to their parents about it.

Maya felt that she could help Shankara meditate more deeply and took it upon herself to encourage him to sit with her and spend time meditating together when they could. She took his hand that day, which he loved, and strolled off the path by the side of a steep, rocky hill one afternoon before the evening meal to a place they had often been. They sat down and crossed their legs, placing the palms of their hands upright in their laps and looking at each other. While they talked, Shankara pulled a long, thin cord from his pocket. As a surprise for Maya, he had several small flowers in his other pocket and started tying them together. She watched intently. Before long he had created a rudimentary bridal flower necklace for her. He gave it to her and blushed. Maya blushed as well.

They both felt a deep fervor in their hearts, a moving feeling, embracing them as eternal friends, a powerful feeling for children. "Namaste," they whispered in unison and closed their eyes momentarily.

As they began their meditation, there was a tremor of the ground, followed by a fast, violent shaking of the earth. Tiny rocks and stones began showering them; a giant boulder rolled over and over from a hundred feet above them on the hillside, gaining speed along with tons of dirt and small trees. Shankara and Maya never saw any of it coming. Just before the quake started, they had taken each other's hands in silence, listening to the cosmic sound of *Om*. He stared into her eye and saw a brilliant light, shaped like a five pointed star.

The earthquake was massive. They were never found.

Chapter Three

The Lemur Man

Madagascar

The fluffy ring-tailed Lemurs of Madagascar have been on the island for countless centuries. The island itself, located in the Indian Ocean off the coast of Africa, is a thousand miles long and about 400 miles wide. The history of Madagascar is distinguished by the early isolation of the landmass from the ancient supercontinents containing Africa and India, and by the island's late colonization of human settlers arriving in outrigger canoes from the Sunda islands between 200 BC and 500 AD. There was a population of Austronesian and Bantu which began to dominate the island before the 1700s.

Manumpana was a very old man who was known in the Malagasy language as the Lemur man. It seemed that any and all Lemurs (which were wild animals) were attracted to the ancient man just as fellow natives were. In fact, people from far away as well as from his own tribe were attracted to him. He had many wives in his life, and too many children to count. His beard was long and white, which was a sign of great wisdom to his people. No one knew how old he was. No one was old enough to remember when he was born, but all understood that he was the oldest and the wisest man on the shores of Madagascar.

He had not a clue of his own age, either. To him, he had always been there, like the trees and the waves and the wind. He had always been aware that he would grow very old. The idea had never bothered him because he foresaw that in his old age, he would not be feeble. And so his vision had come true. He was not feeble, and, even though he lived on a diet of rice for most of his life, he had lean, strong muscles. Although Malagasy people were poor, and many ate meat, Manumpana had never in his life killed or eaten a living thing; he thought his God would not like the idea for him. He felt this inclination came from his ancestors as well.

His greatest strength came in his spiritual awareness. Although as a young man, he very vaguely remembered that he wanted to be a warrior, he had given up on that dream many years before and intuitively followed a spiritual path to better understand why he existed and what his mission in life was destined to be.

All the Malagasy people traditionally accepted the existence of a supreme God, known commonly as Zanahary (Creator) or Andriamanitra (Sweet, or Fragrant, Lord). The dead were conceived as playing the role of intermediary between this supreme God and humankind and viewed as having the power to affect the destinies of those still living.

Manumpana was a high soul, and living his life to do good for others had been his lifelong aspiration and eventually the destiny in his locally illustrious life. It had proven to be the essence of happiness for him.

The burial tomb, a prominent part of the island's landscape in all regions, is the primary link between the living and the dead among the Malagasy people. It is built with great care and expense, reflecting the privileged position of the dead, and is often more costly and substantial than the houses of the living.

Manumpana's home was a very humble but sturdy shack, which withstood the monsoon seasons year after year. It was near his first wife, Moona's, burial tomb, the woman he loved the most. She was attractive by Malagasy standards but had an unusual feature; her left eye was locked in a position that made it always appear to be looking to the right. It didn't matter to her, as she was blind in that eye and there were no mirrors, only reflections in the still lake, which she avoided.

Manumpana's shack was a fine home for him and his Lemur friends. Islanders would come to visit the Lemur man and ask questions of the past and future and sometimes for healing blessings. Some of them were his children or their children or their children's children. He was never absolutely sure who they were, except the ones from Moona; they looked like her, but he loved them all equally. His advice in most cases was pretty much the same. "Make others happy, and keep Zanahary here" (and he would point to the place on his forehead between his eyes). "Always. And when the ancestors come for you to join them, they will recognize you are royalty as you move forward in your spiritual unfoldment."

Manumpana was also famous far and wide for his drumming. He played an instrument called a djembe, a rope-tuned, skin–covered, goblet drum. According to the Bamanan people of Mali, the name of the djembe came from a saying which meant, "Everyone gather together in peace." And when people gathered around Manumpana to listen to his enchanting rhythm on the djembe, the experience defined the drums and the purpose of Manumpana's life.

After he eventually made his final transition through the thin wall between the living and the dead, a village was named after him, Manumpana. His legend was timeless, and many Malagasy were saved from great fear by following his advice. They followed his counsel by focusing on their God as much as they could. They lived busy lives of bare survival on an island that could never produce enough food or commerce to keep the entire population alive or increasing in numbers.

Although Manumpana knew his soul would be carried through his departure from life on Madagascar, he did not know where his next incarnation would be. He knew only that if he would fulfill his current mission of bringing peace to all who knew him, he would become old and honored as he so desired. Near the end, he dreamed he was a spiritual warrior and that he was white. He had never seen such a thing in his life.

He also had a vision of being with Moona again. And she was white, too, but her eye was normal. He could not imagine why God would bleach the natural color of skin to a sickly, pale white. He knew visions were dreams, some true and some passing fantasies, but given his great spiritual intuition, deep in his prayers, he was reassured that he would be with his beloved soul-mate, Moona, again, somewhere, sometime.

The night he died, there was a brutal monsoon. He was snuggling in his straw bed with several lemurs, their furry tails wrapped around him. He went into a deep sleep, with his eyes concentrating on the spot in his forehead between his bushy, white eyebrows. He saw a bright white star brilliantly glowing, and he smiled as he floated above the cot and his dead body. The Lemurs were nervous, their eyes flashing back and forth between their departed host and the ghostly image of him above the body. Suddenly one squealed, and they all began squealing and scampering away. In the bay, several whales made the same noise, as if talking to the lemurs, which they had been doing for thousands of years. The ghost of Manumpana slowly dissipated as it floated through the top of the shack straight upwards, despite the gale force wind which quickly dismantled the shack and blew out to sea.

The crew of lemur troops had found shelter under a fallen tree and watched the last semblance of their beloved friend vanish, but not from their loyal little hearts.

Manumpana lived a good life and suffered not in his final departure. He knew Andriamanitra would guide him into his assigned place beyond the living. To bless the old man's journey further, she took the form of a lemur and led his little friends back into the mangrove forest to safety until the monsoon had passed.

Chapter Four

Daniel

Tennessee, USA

Colonel Daniel Draper was loved by everyone who ever met him. Officers revered him; enlisted men saw him as an individual deserving both his rank and the respect of the troops under his command. He was a stocky, muscular man with a red and grey beard. He had wanted to be a soldier since long before there was a Continental Army.

April 1775 kicked off the armed conflict, and by the following summer, the rebels were waging a full-scale war for American independence. Before long it seemed as though Daniel had served an entire lifetime as a career soldier in the Continental Army, but, for the most part, it had not hardened him or tainted his sweet disposition. His weakness was that of many men finally caught up in a war that seemed as though it would go on forever. Sour mash whiskey was his drink of choice. But where it made other men angry and pugnacious, it made him mellow for the most part. There had been two occasions when insults had been exchanged, and each time Daniel simply rendered his heckler unconscious. Men knew Colonel Dan as a great soldier, compassionate, but with emotions that were not to be toyed with on any level.

Although hunting was a necessity, Daniel somehow felt that he had developed a bad habit of taking some pleasure in shooting animals. Just seeing their demise or being responsible for their death was not right with him on some level, and although he would eat meat occasionally, he didn't really like it. Deep down, he felt guilty. He didn't know why he felt that way, but the whisky helped him forget it. Other men had no compunction about shooting critters for fun. To Daniel, it seemed wrong. He just felt differently about it, but rarely talked to anyone about his feelings except his beloved Emma.

Emma Jane was a staunch Baptist, known to all to be stern. Folks in general figured Daniel had more respect for her authority than he did for General Mumsford, his commanding officer. But she was lovely beyond words, and behind closed doors, her apparently cool and sometimes aloof attitude was passionately dismantled by the very touch of her loving husband's hand. There was a characteristic that moved Danny in a way he could not explain. Emma would lie back on their feather bed and blink her azure blue eyes seductively, and then with her right eye wide open, she would close her left eye, not winking but just leaving it closed for a minute as if to say, *Come love me, my darling*. And make love they did, on countless nights. The trait was beguiling, unique, and totally involuntary; something clicked in Emma's head, and her eye would lock down for a minute or two. Daniel thought it was the sexiest wink he had ever seen or would ever see. The passion they shared was as it was meant to be, the ultimate fulfillment of a love that seemed as though it had been going on forever: sublimely physical and simultaneously deeply spiritual, a divine commitment on all levels.

Danny believed that nothing could ever separate them, and Emma confirmed that idea through her faith that with Christ the savior, they would be in heaven together for eternity. Daniel loved to listen to Emma read scripture. He wanted to debate the logic of much of it with her, but knew that it was indeed the way, the truth and the life for her. *So be it*, he thought to himself. One time he said, "Emma, whether we are together in heaven or live another life here on earth, we will be together forever."

This approach didn't work with Emma. For her, the Bible was the word of God, and "There shall be no life after death on this planet, only on streets paved with gold beyond the pearly gates of Paradise, where we will hold hands and sing hymns in praise of the Lord."

Religious debates never lasted long, especially on the nights before Danny left on a mission. It was an unspoken promise that they were always the most passionate times, and at the same time the saddest. The outcome of the upcoming days or weeks was always an uncertain mystery, missions fraught with ghastly danger. Colonel Daniel was fearless, feeling that God was with him whenever he had to leave on an assignment.

Their union had brought them one lovely daughter whom they both adored, their wise, little three-year-old, Camille. She, too, seemed to sense when Daniel was leaving for something more than just a visit to town or other daily business. She didn't want to let go of her daddy when a mission was imminent.

Such a night came about, and in the morning Emma was even more uneasy than usual. She served cornbread and grits and then many long, soft kisses before taking Camille to stand on the porch of their cabin in Gatlinburg, Tennessee, as Colonel Danny mounted his huge horse, Troy, pulled the reins to the right, threw a kiss to them, and was galloping north towards Yorktown, Virginia. It was 1779.

Emma and Daniel felt the war had turned in favor of the Continental Army after the French had joined the fray in 1778 and that the end was in sight. Once back on the battlefield Colonel Daniel was soon in the middle of it all. He began to run into officers and men coming his way. "Can't stop 'em, Sir!" shouted a soldier. "There must be a thousand of 'em."

The Colonel understood fighting against the odds and knew that it was now a balancing act in what he figured was the final stages of the war of independence. As waves of more of his troops and civilians fleeing the enemy kept coming his way, he noticed a small child huddled up against a pine tree just off the trail. He yanked the reins and pulled Troy towards the tree, where he threw his leg over the front of the saddle and landed on both feet solidly a few feet from the child. He could see now that it was a girl wrapped in gingham, and instantly he thought of his beloved Camille. As he knelt down, he could hear shells exploding and the sound of fighting getting closer. He looked up to see if any of the redcoats were in sight. The blast of a cap and ball rifle alerted him that the enemy was closer than he thought.

He pulled down his army blanket and wrapped the child firmly, thinking of his darling Camille again and how this baby was equally important to the world. He glanced closer at her precious face and smiled. As he tried to grab the reins on the ground, another shot whizzed by, and Troy, his powerful horse, bolted for the trail.

The Colonel could hear the agonized hollering and screaming of battle and knew the bastard redcoats were advancing swiftly. His experience in the field and military intuition told him that, as he had only one shot in his pistol, it would soon be hand to hand, sword to sword combat with the enemy. But he also knew he would possess the power of an army of one with God behind him.

He stood up, swearing to himself that no harm would come to the little girl. He gently placed her against the stump of the tree, threw his hat down, and prayed to Jesus to stand beside him in his defense of the child.

He also had a flask of whiskey he had carried but not touched in weeks. He quickly withdrew it and downed the last half of it. He felt the burning in his throat and belly and took a deep breath.

"For God and country and this holy child!" he screamed and threw the bottle off to the opposite side of the trees in the clearing. Suddenly, for a second, he felt like this scene had happened to him before, a déjà vu.

War creates monsters in battle. And it's not even their fault; they are people who have been thrown into the most unimaginable and heinous scenarios on earth. Danny was ready, facing the coming dragoons, and he was riled, furious. His steel blue eyes glistened with anger; if he had to die, then let it be, but by God, the little girl would live.

Three British regulars came out of the brush, charging him. They didn't even notice the child. The first one shot and winged the Colonel in the left shoulder.

"Wrong shoulder!" Dan shouted as he pulled his pistol out with his right hand and fired dead center at the chest of the intruder.

"One down," he yelled at the other two, who were now approaching full speed with a vengeance.

"Lord!" he shouted. "Lord God, stay with me; don't let this baby die!" And he heard a voice in his head different than any sound he ever heard. "The child will live."

One British solder met the rapid slash of the Colonel's sword across his neck. Spurting blood in all directions, he fell quickly.

"One to go!" screamed Colonel Daniel. As he spun around, the two were squared off and exchanging parries faster than either knew they could move.

A slash to the left leg brought Danny to the ground as he continued to fight the battle from there. The enemy was a big, shaggy-headed man with a nasty, sadistic grin. He kept slashing, cutting Danny superficially but with deadly intent.

Danny was losing blood and feeling dizzy; he was losing the battle. But in one last flurry, he rolled to the left and kicked the leg of the soldier out from underneath him with his right leg. But the shaggy-headed soldier quickly rebounded, laughing and screaming obscenities as he advanced again.

"Don't touch this child!" screamed the Colonel, as he fought from the ground and scooted back to prop himself up against the tree over the girl. His body covered hers. Blood gushed both from his shoulder wounds and his savagely mangled left leg.

"You revolutionary pig!" shouted the British soldier, who had still not even noticed the girl. He lunged downward, thrusting his sword fully into Daniel's left kidney. Colonel Daniel Draper felt nothing as he watched his wounds spitting blood. As his sight faded, he saw only the eyes of Emma, the left one closed and the right one open, and he heard her saintly voice saying, "Sweet dreams, my love," as she had so many times.

His eyes blinked, and a burst of sunlight revealed two of his men taking down the rebel by hand and knife. "The baby is safe," said the voice in his head.

Daniel smiled; the pain was excruciating for a fraction of a second. Then there was brilliant light and what sounded like a host of angels; a waterfall of a thousand lifetimes flooded his head and tumbled like an avalanche into an eternal star field.

At thirty-eight years old, the honorable Colonel Daniel Draper lay dead . . . but not forgotten.

Chapter Five

Dieter

Atlantic Ocean

A still sea and gulls drifting with the subtle breezes were diametrically different from the horrendous storm that had sunk Baron Helmsley's yacht so quickly the day before.

And now the scene was ironically placid, as is the fickle way of the Atlantic Ocean. Searching for lost private luxury vessels in the late 1700's was unheard of unless a ship was hired to do so.

The wooden railing of the already weather-worn, nine meter life raft was an ideal perch for the seagulls, hundreds of miles from land. They seemed to be casually picking at different things in the boat, when an enormous Laysan albatross with a wingspan almost as wide as the length of the boat glided in easily, scattering the startled gulls. Before it settled on the edge by the broken oar, the seagulls had taken flight. The feathery giant flapped its muscular wings, and then lowered its mighty beak to poke at the body on the floor of the boat.

Suddenly, from the apparently lifeless body of the one human survivor, a seaman's knife jabbed upwards into the breast of the bird. Blood spurted out, along with a belly full of salt water. (Albatrosses actually drink salt water.)

As the gigantic bird fought for its life, the man now had a grip on its neck, and, with his large, strong left hand and a surge of strength, he sliced the neck like a professional butcher. The bird fell on top of him, and he had just enough strength left to push it aside as he lay exhausted and confused.

"Gott n Himmel!" (God in Heaven!) mumbled the big man with a gravelly, hoarse voice. His eyes were wide and ghastly bloodshot. "Wasser," (water), he croaked, realizing his enormous thirst.

Dieter was as thirsty as he had ever been, confused and dehydrated. The giant bird began to twitch. Without thinking, he shouted "Halt," and, as if it understood, the mammoth bird stopped moving. So did Dieter, as he passed out next to it. A spectacular sunset made the grisly scene uncanny. Night fell, and Dieter Bauer lay very still next to a bird that weighed almost as much as he did.

Dieter fell into a very deep sleep. He was with his wondrous girlfriend Layna (dreaming of the night they met). He had been drinking a new lager with his friends that night, when she walked into the Frandorfer gasthaus, and all jaws dropped open. As the largest man in the place, he easily pushed forward, staring at the beautiful Deutsch blonde and said, "You look like an angel."

"That's what my name, Layna, means . . . Angel."

Dieter, a confirmed atheist, said, "Now I believe in God." And he meant it.

They became lovers the first night, and were together day and night from that point on for four years. Why he ever agreed to help his friend Baron Helmsley crew for his yacht against her wishes, he would never know. But now he was back beside her in the soft, downy comfort of his bed. He was looking in her endless, ocean-blue eyes. And as if he weren't already aroused, she would wink, and a surge of blood pulsed through his entire body. The simple wink had an unreal effect on him emotionally. He ran his left hand over her full breasts and down her side, along her lovely, incredibly silky, smooth hip.

"Ich liebe dich," (I love you,) she whispered. "Ich vierede dich immer lieben." (I will always love you.)

He rolled over to face her, her hot, panting breath and wet lips arousing him beyond belief. He began to pet her hip again and slipped his hand between her long, muscular legs. She whispered softly "Iragathnued."

"What?" he asked.

Then she spoke loudly, yelling in his face, "EGESACKXMAT!" And she ran the finger nails from her right hand into his throat.

He screamed in terror and jerked back. It was the bird's foot in his throat. Was it still alive? As he scrambled in the dim light of dawn, the bird's blood was all over him, sticky and cold. He was frantic. He was on his hands and knees and then standing up, shaking the whole boat. He tried to get a grip and was staring at the corpse of the hideous albatross like a madman.

He heard the flock of squawking petrels flying above, which had sensed the dead albatross and began diving in for a closer look.

"Vasser!" screamed Dieter. His throat was parched so that he could hardly speak. But he could swing an oar, which he did, knocking down two petrels with his first swing. As the sun rose, he battled the petrels that were relentlessly after the albatross and pecking him, too, when they could. Near total and complete exhaustion, he decided to give the albatross to the obdurate petrels. After several difficult moves, taking virtually all his remaining energy, he finally dumped the lifeless body in the ocean. The monstrous bird floated away, and the petrels began picking on it voraciously, with a few still coming at Dieter in the flurry.

Dieter grabbed the good paddle and aimed the boat away from them. He kept paddling and mumbling, "Ich liebe dich, Layna," and then, in a fading whisper, "Vasser, vasser, vasser. Jai Krishna. Jai Krishna."

Hours passed; it was twilight. Dieter was delirious and hadn't thought of food, just water. But now his growling stomach spoke up; he looked around and saw four dead petrels that must have met his oar earlier. He was looking for his knife, and as he picked up a bloody blanket, he found a flask of water.

"A miracle!" he thought. He took a swig and realized it was brandy. He started to gag and forced himself to swallow. It burned his throat all the way to his empty stomach. He smiled an insane smile, put the cork in the bottle and passed out again.

He dreamed. It was a humid day in the woods somewhere by a rocky hillside, a place he had never been in his homeland. Dieter was now a small child sitting with a little girl with one eye missing. She was indeed a beautiful child, with dark skin, a clef chin and deep dimples when she smiled. He looked at his hands, and they were dark, too. He felt so warm and wonderful sitting there with this strange girl, who felt like an old friend. They were sitting cross-legged, facing each other and holding hands.

"Namaste," she said.

"Vas meinst du?" (What do you mean?) he said, smiling, and then the ground started shaking. They just stared at each other.

"Jai Krishna," she said quickly. "Meditate with me, Shankara. Say 'Jai Krishna, Jai Krishna, Jai Krishna,' please, over and over, say it."

"Ya, Jai Krishna, Jai Krishna," he replied, shaking his head in disbelief. "Ach, mein Gott," (Oh, my God), it was an earthquake!

He woke up to face a wall of water; the boat was in a swell. The tiny raft was on the top of a wave and then barreling down the other side. Leaning back on the only seat in the boat, as the spray thoroughly soaked him, again and again he screamed, "Layna,

Layna, Layna, Layna," then trailed off. He stood up, hands in the air, crying for help, and was thrown forward like a rag doll. He landed in the front of the boat, smacking his head on the side rail and was knocked unconscious.

The dawn brought another placid, serene scenario. Still unbearably hot and humid, another day passed in the calm sea. He didn't wake up. Then it was morning again, and he was lying on his back. Pain seared through his head, and his throat was as dry as cactus. Too parched to swallow, he could just barely hear a man's voice, speaking French. It must be another dream, he thought.

"Bonjour, mon ami." (Good morning, my friend.)

Dieter felt a hand behind his head, tilting it forward, and then the blessed drops of fresh water being carefully administered to his pale and cracked lips. The sun was too bright for him to focus, but he slowly imbibed the water with the help of the apparent good samaritan who was carefully bracing him to receive the life-giving liquid. Ever so slowly, Dieter started to come around.

Just as he became aware that they were in the sunlight, they floated into the cool relief of a shadow. What actually happened was that the huge French fishing barge tanker had moved slightly as the wind had picked up a bit.

Captain Henry La Beuff was the older Frenchman who had lowered himself to the raft and had apparently been sitting with Dieter for some time before he gained consciousness enough to know that water had been dripped slowly on his brow and his lips to awaken him. Dieter was battered and bloody, partly from his falls and partly because of the gory albatross, which had surely become fish and bird food many hours before.

The barge/tanker, clearly a customized vessel, was called *Une Nymphe Marine,* meaning in mythology, a beautiful maiden of the sea. It took two surly ship hands and Henry La Beuff to help Dieter up the rope ladder to the deck of the Nymphe. It was a very large, flat, barge-like ship, like nothing Dieter had ever seen before. It had two smokestacks in addition to one sail in front and another one aft, plus what Dieter thought was a jib sail off the bow.

Everything was a blur, and he was so weak, the men practically had to carry him to a cabin. It was a small, filthy room near the rear part of the vessel, behind the last huge smokestack.

Dieter had never claimed to be sailor, but even if he had been, he could not have identified what kind of ship this was. It was one of a kind. He would learn to know much more about the hideous craft over the coming months, months that would become the most torturous and agonizing of his life.

The one thing that assailed his senses in the beginning and continued to accost his senses for the entire trip was the hogs, the enormous pigs Captain La Beuff was transporting to the Sandwich Islands. Their feces could never be shoved overboard fast enough. It was only because of the ocean trade winds that there was any occasional relief to the nostrils of the mangy, enslaved crew. The nonstop squealing of the monstrous hogs added to the nightmare on what Dieter began to think of as a ghost ship.

La Beuff had seemed kind, gentle, and even happy when he helped Dieter in the beginning. Dieter was soon to find out that he was simply pleased to have another crew member, one who didn't have to be shanghaied.

Most of the men were down and out drunks, literally picked up off the streets of bars and brothels around the harbors of Europe, several escaped slaves, some Chinese, some white men, and many of mixed race.

Dieter Bauer might have been eaten by sharks or predatory birds had he not been rescued by La Beuff; yet more than once he wished that had been his fate. Soon he was just one of the mangy crew, ruled by three hideous, heartless, strong-armed bullies, who were recruited from slave ships because of their "talents" with handling men, as La Beuff explained to Dieter with a sickening grin.

The crew was kept on a near-starvation diet of hardtack. When La Beuff and his cronies felt the crew was close to death, they would slaughter a pig. The men were fed like animals on the deck after the slaughtered pigs were thrown onto a controlled feeding area on the deck. These were miserable, sick men, all living day to day in the worst conditions imaginable. Not one had escaped; most had scurvy and other untold infections and diseases. It was a living hell.

Dieter had been raised in an upper middle class home in his beloved K-town. He was a spoiled, only child who never learned to give to another or to believe in any power greater than himself. On occasion he did feel some guilt for his self-centeredness, but never chose to do anything about it.

He'd lived with that attitude until he had met Layna. She magically changed his life. She was a Buddhist, which meant nothing to him at first. But to know her was to admire and love whatever spiritual path she followed. When she told him he would reach "Nirvana" (a kind of heaven) through deep meditation and kind acts, then that became his goal. She explained karma to him, that the bad things that he did in his life or his prior life would come back to haunt him, and that the good or righteous acts would save him from great fear and retribution. She had told him, "The way you live and the way you help others will determine your destiny, dear Dieter. In the next life, we will be in a paradise of perfect food, warm weather, always sunny, with sandy beaches and gentle breezes." She would look upward and speak even more softly, "That will be our Nirvana, Dieter; we will be together forever."

Deep down, Dieter had felt that would never happen, but he adored the dream.

She so mesmerized Dieter when he was with her that he believed her every word at the time. She was also mesmerized by him. The mutual effect had been life-altering for them both.

She truly caused him to change in a dramatic way. His parents and his friends all knew she was a divine influence and were forever grateful to her. They also agreed that Angel was a perfect name for her.

Layna had begged him not to go on Baron Helmsley's yacht, but Dieter still hung on to some of his selfish ways and went to "have a good time," even though as he boarded the yacht and looked back at Layna with an undying love in his heart, he knew that it might be the last time he would see her, except in his dreams.

He sat on the deck with tears pouring down his filthy face as he remembered the Elysian Layna and thought of her angel-soft skin. Then the bloody albatross appeared in his mind, and he screamed.

Few of the men even looked up as they fed slop to the pigs and shoved their waste overboard. Men periodically screamed, and on three occasions charged to the edge of barge and threw themselves overboard. Nobody except Dieter cared when this happened.

At first Dieter simply suffered as the days and months dragged on. And then in the midst of all the agony, Layna's precise words came back to him, he closed his eyes and heard her voice clearly and it changed him forever, *There's an ancient creed illuminating trials we face, that as you give your love, so measured is your Grace."*

The words were indelible in his mind. He knew he would probably die on the ship, and yet, even in his own dire circumstances, he became determined to help the other men however he could. He was the biggest and strongest of them and in much better shape, as they were all emaciated and had been for a long time before he was ever aboard the grisly ship.

Dieter would offer part of his meager rations to others and come to their aid when they were hopeless and in pain and anguish. On two occasions he actually intercepted men from leaping overboard. On other occasions he carried men who might not have lived to the Captain and convinced La Beuff to help him save their lives. Captain La Beuff had nothing but selfish motives in anything he did, so Dieter convinced him that helping the men was to his best advantage, since they would live to work longer.

Dieter even discovered that La Beuff had secret supplies and stores of food for himself and his jackal henchmen. Both La Beuff and Dieter spoke English and eventually developed a rapport of sorts. La Beuff invited Dieter into his cabin for meals sometimes, another reason Dieter was surviving better than the other men. But Dieter was also able to steal bits and pieces of hardtack and dried fruit, risking his own life to feed others who needed it to survive. The men called him "Dok," short for doktor. Even the sickest of them felt that his smile and his help gave them hope in the face of the worst adversity.

Dieter would lie half awake at night in the straw, repeating to himself, "Jai Krishna, Jai Krishna, Jai Krishna." He didn't know why. Or he'd say, "Buddha, Nirvana; Buddha, Nirvana; Buddha,

Nirvana." All he knew was that Layna would want him to pray and told him that if he did, blessings would come his way.

Every once in a while, he would also pray to Jesus, as he was taught as a child: "Dear Jesus, please save me from this hideous life."

He always slept deeply and in spite of intolerable conditions, gave of himself to the dying men of the doomed *Une Nymphe Marine.* Many times he would gather a few men together and pray. Since he had no formal idea of how to pray, he would just start with "Dear Jesus" and then mention the men's names and tell them that the son of God was with them in their trials. His prayers never varied much, but they brought a sense of calmness and serenity to a doomed crew on a cruise to hell.

It was a miracle that the ship survived as it endured horrible storms around Cape Horn, and conditions on board got worse as the time wore on, beyond comprehension. Whipping the men was a common practice. On a few occasions Dieter actually grabbed the brute doing the whipping and physically stopped him, saving men's lives. Only because he had become La Beuff's only intelligent company was he himself not whipped.

Intolerably long humid days of the agony, abuse, starvation and hopelessness seemed endless to the battered and dying men of *Une Nymphe Marine.* It seemed like a miracle to the shanghaied crew that Dieter kept a positive attitude and lifted the men with lightheartedness, prayer and song. But Dieter was running on empty. As he stared out at infinity across the ocean, it seemed that the eternal stillness of the sea was but a precursor to an abysmal end. The men seemed desperate and although literally dying of hunger and thirst, were restless with outrageous anxiety. Mutiny madness was brewing.

As a hurricane came roaring across the Pacific Ocean, the men had all reached the end of their rope and were already in the process of attacking La Beuff and his slave beaters. After overwhelming them, they threw the bodies into the pigpens, where they were trampled upon and eaten.

As the violent sea began to be more turbulent than ever, the men began leaping overboard. When the force of the hurricane piled into *Une Nymphe Marine,* it tore the ship to splinters.

Then suddenly, after all the death and destruction was over, the sea was still and flat again.

To foreigners like the Europeans in the late 1800s, Hawaii was known as the Sandwich Islands. But to the natives it was simply and always would be Hawaii. La Beuff had intended to deliver his enormous hogs to a buyer in Lahaina, a famous whaling village on the island of Maui. His ship never made it. Ultimately the huge pigs that did begin to inhabit the islands as a result of shipments like La Beuff's began to escape and run wild, causing endless problems. Decimating the under story of the native Hawaiian forests over the years, they caused the greatest ecological damage of any of the invasive ungulates, consuming everything from plants to fungi to carrion.

The haggard body of the once powerful Dieter Bauer had been pushed onto a large piece of decking by three fellow slaves who had learned to love and respect Dok. They had all gripped the deck plank tenaciously during the hurricane, but Dieter was the only one strong enough to cling to it and never relent. They had willingly saved his life but lost their own, and in their dying, they felt a blessing for an altruism that changed their own karmic destinies.

As the waves on the black sand beach of Honokalani sloshed up and pushed the board around, his body was washed off, and he lay motionless on his back. As the Maui sun beat down on his tormented, nearly naked body, a shadow was cast over him. He was not aware. It was an enormous effort just to mumble, "Jai Krishna, Jai Krishna, Jai Krishna." He felt a gentle hand under his head and tried to open his eyes, but at first it was impossible. He was in a delirious dream state.

"Layna, my love; Layna, is that you?"

"Shhhhhh," was the response he heard.

As he began to squint enough to see, there she was, bare breasted, kneeling beside him and smiling like the angel she was. Was the sunlight playing tricks, or was she playfully winking at him? He couldn't be sure then.

"Layna, thank God!"

He blinked again and again; his eyes were filled with sand, dried seawater, and tears. She gently dripped fresh coconut juice into his mouth and lightly touched his severely parched lips with the same liquid. He was still delirious, yet coming around. Layna was more beautiful than ever with a dark tan, dimples, clef chin, and ever priceless beauty. But her hair was not blonde; it was a long, shiny black now, as black as the sand.

"Layna, oh, Layna, is this Nirvana?"

She didn't answer. Everything was blurry, but he knew this was not a dream. She was real; even if her hair was black, it was surely Layna.

"Aloha," she said.

He was in heaven. "Layna, oh, Layna, you are so gorgeous;" his voice was barely audible. But she didn't understand his language, only felt his ardor.

He could see more clearly now as she leaned closer to his face, pointed to herself, and said, "Leilani . . . Lei!" She pointed to the plumeria lei she had around her neck.

"Lay," he repeated, smiling. "Lay, I love it; I love you, Lay."

She smiled, seemed to wink again, and gently pulled his sun-scorched head against her naked breast amongst the fragrant garlands. Dieter was in heaven. He fell asleep as she rocked back and forth, singing an island song that meant, *You are loved.* And his senses were filled with the earthy scent of a woman and the aromatic plumaria around Lei's neck, feeling the heavenly body of an Angel caressing him, his face against her breast like a baby in his mother's arms.

It was weeks before he began to recover. Nourished on wild herbs, papayas, mangoes, mountain apples, bananas, and Lei's love, he finally was made to understand that he had reached the Sandwich Islands. And Lei was not really Layna, but to him, she was, and they had reached heaven, Nirvana, together.

The missionaries were getting well positioned in the islands for the eventual takeover of the palace in Honolulu in 1893. But on this far end of Maui, near modern day Hana, few foreigners were ever seen. Accidentally, a wandering German Catholic priest encountered Dieter living with Layna and her family. He interpreted many Hawaiian words and wrote them down, explaining to Dieter much of what had been a mystery to him. The kindly missionary also offered to take him back to a place called Makawoa with him, saying, "We don't come here too often, and we have a lovely stone cathedral in Makawoa, and the natives here are. . . terribly primitive." He was staring at Lei's naked breasts as he spoke.

Dieter assured him he would be fine and thanked him for his help. The priest said, "I am concerned for your eternal soul, my son!"

"It is in good shape, Father; I am in Nirvana." The priest, of course, did not understand.

"Jai Krishna, Father." Dieter knew that would confuse the priest, too, so he smiled. "I am here in heaven, Father, and I will stay here with Lei. I will never leave. Aloha. Be assured my soul is in good hands."

"I don't understand," said Father O'Brien.

Dieter grinned and remembered something else Layna had taught him: "Good Karma, unt Danke" (thank you).

Dieter and Lei had three keiki (children). They were all vegetarians. Some natives hunted and ate the wild deer and even the pigs, but Dieter could not even be around when the wild pigs were cooking; the smell made him sick. He warned the natives against eating the heinous animals but usually to no avail. Eventually many diseases began to decimate the native population to a fraction of the 800,000 who were there in the mid 1800s.

Dieter became a great ukulele player. He would play and Lei would sing and dance the traditional hula. He also became very proficient at playing the puniu (coconut shell knee drum) he felt he had been playing his whole life. He made mele (music, song, prayers and poetical chants) and, in time, the natives accepted him as a brother and called him Kimo. Lei said it meant *strong warrior* in her ancestors' family.

Dieter had changed through the tribulations of his horrid journey. He believed that the hardships were trials that made him stronger and more spiritual in every way and ultimately a better man.

Until the day he died, he continued to help others and to feel blessed for every day of his life with Lei and his keiki near the black sand beach he and Lei called "Nirvana."

By the way he ultimately led his life, he became what the Hindus call a karma Yogi.

Chapter Six

Justin

Portland, Oregon USA

Sweet Hannah May's heavenly voice was the pride of the Presbyterian congregation. She was only sixteen, lovely beyond words, and her boyfriend, Justin Daniels, was a perfect match for her. Not only was he tall and handsome, but he was also a fine guitar player and accompanied Hannah May on hymns from the classic Olney Hymnbook used in most churches in America starting in the early 1800s. Hannah May had long, naturally curly, blonde hair. Justin didn't sing, but when he played for Hannah May, she would stand on the steps above him, and as he looked up at her with the light of the stained glass window behind her, she appeared to be an angel with a heavenly halo. His heart always skipped a beat or two.

The most popular hymn of the day was the timeless classic AMAZING GRACE written by John Newton, published in the late 1700s. Justin took great pride in strumming his James Ashborn parlor style guitar, which his late father had left him. He felt he was born with rhythm, demonstrated in a unique style in which he would thump and tap on his guitar as much as strum it, which world travelers had told him gave it a tribal sound. Others would say disdainfully that it sounded like black gospel music. Personally, he had a great affinity for black music and didn't really care what people said. He liked the sounds he produced, and no matter what anyone said, he knew most everyone else seemed to like his music, especially when Hannah May was singing, at which time his guitar-playing was the perfect accompaniment.

The folks at the Presbyterian Church of Portland, Oregon, enjoyed the service partly because of the Reverend Zachariah's fire and brimstone delivery, as it was powerful and spiritually uplifting. But most folks relied on the blessed Hannah May's singing with Justin Daniels accompanying her. The church organ had not arrived from New England yet. As time went on, the parishioners felt perhaps the Reverend Zachariah had never really sent the money for it. There was a rumor that he spent time with the "devil rum" when he was far from the pulpit. But nobody could prove it; nobody ever sensed the smell of booze on his breath. It was just a rumor. They did know he liked a party and would roll out his fiddle for his favorite tune, *Turkey in the Straw*, sometimes at picnics or hoedowns.

Justin was totally enchanted by Hannah May. She had his number. He was the only man she ever seductively winked at, and she knew how it affected him. But it wasn't just a wink, it was a kind of twitch. Whatever it was, she didn't do it for anyone else; it drove him wild, and she knew it. So in public she did it whenever no one could see. Whether she was singing to him or melting in his arms as he pressed her body against a tree in the forest in their secret place west of town, they knew they were made for each other in every way. The loving couple would spend hours in such embraces and endless, wet kisses, and fondling one another.

How they managed, they didn't know, only that by Christian ethics they should not have intercourse until they were married; therefore they never actually made love out of wedlock.

One time after an afternoon of such deep passion in the woods, Justin helped Hannah May into his ranch buckboard to head back to town. Suddenly, the horse bolted before he got to the other side, and it took off. It happened so fast that before he knew it, he could see Hannah turning back and screaming over her shoulder.

He hollered, "Grab the reigns, Hannah!"

She shook her head hopelessly, so he screamed louder, "Grab the reigns, Hannah; pull them!"

Hannah rode well but never handled a buckboard much. Justin began to run full tilt towards the disappearing wagon. When Hannah finally grabbed the reigns from her side and yanked hard, the horse swung his head to the right and cranked the wagon into almost jackknifing. Now it was heading back to some degree, and Justin adjusted the angle of his run in order to try to catch up with the careening buckboard. He had never run so hard in his life, but he was very strong and fast and moved like a seasoned athlete. Hannah May kept pulling the reigns with her left hand, while trying to hang on to the steel handle by the right side of the wooden seat.

Just as Justin reached the wagon, Hannah yanked again, and the wagon did jackknife airborne, landing upside down on Justin. Hannah May was thrown free, and landed on her knees and elbows.

She didn't feel the pain or see the blood. She staggered to her feet to find her love. She suddenly realized that he was trapped underneath the wagon. The horse lay motionless.

The wagon, fortunately, was not a flatbed and had pine planks along both sides; the back was open. Hannah May bent down and yelled into the back of the overturned rig, "Justin, oh, honey, where are you?"

There was no sound, and at first she couldn't see under the wagon because the hot, Oregon, summer sun was so bright. As she lay on her belly and began to crawl in, she could see his foot and then his right leg. She knew she couldn't get in beside him, so she turned over and, lying on her side, braced both legs on one of the two by fours holding the sides up. Lying on her left side now, she grabbed Justin's boot. Still repeating frantically, "Justin, Justin, Justin, talk to me, darling," trying desperately to pull him by the boot, the boot came off. She threw it back and grabbed his ankle with both hands and pulled with all her might.

"Oh, dear God, please. . . my darling, Justin. Please, God; Oh, Jesus, we love you, Jesus; save my man, don't let him die." She kept praying out loud as she slowly but surely straightened her legs and pulled him part way out. She still couldn't see his face, so she repositioned herself outside the wagon on her knees, pulling on both legs with one under each arm, completely unaware of the blood that dripped from her elbows and knees. One final Herculean effort, and she pulled him into the light. She quickly dropped herself down right next to his motionless body. His face was as white as a sheet with a stark, red gash across his cheek.

With her arm slid under his neck and her other hand on his chest, she felt no heart beat. Tears burst from her eyes like a storm front and poured down her flushed cheeks. "Oh, God; oh, sweet Jesus, not Justin, not my Justin; God, Jesus, please, I swear I will sing my sweetest for you forever if you just save my sweet Justin. . ."

She swallowed hard, cradling his limp body tightly. She cleared her throat and began singing softly, as if to God personally, her angelic voice as soft as velvet, "Amazing Grace, how sweet thou art . . ."

Justin hadn't felt anything after he dove to try and avoid the flying wagon. There was no pain when it hit him. He knew the wagon had landed on top of him and that he was lying on his back. He tilted his head up and could see his legs and the light at the end of the wagon. And then there was an infinite void of blackness and a star-filled sky. He wondered, "How can I see the sky if there is a wagon on top of me?" And then he stopped thinking as the most brilliant star in the sky was coming at him. It was a glorious green.

And then suddenly he was sitting in a grass shack surrounded by a group of people he assumed were southern slaves. They were smiling and clapping their hands along with his own bare, calloused hands, beating a strange drum in his lap. The drum was made of a skin-covered shell. He marveled at it, feeling the joy he felt when he played for Hannah May. He looked up at a woman in the circle; it was

Hannah May, and she was black. He didn't notice that his own skin was black, too. And there were a number of strange little animals that appeared to be half raccoon and half cat with long black and white striped tails (lemurs); they sat up on their back legs and began clapping, too.

Justin blinked, shook his head in confusion, and found himself standing upright below the star field again. He felt fantastic, and then he was facing a light so bright that he shielded his eyes with his arm. He began to walk toward it, a warm feeling surging through his body and drawing him toward the light. The ground was a golden hue. "It's heaven," he thought, "I am in heaven; I must be holding hands with Hannah May."

And then he did feel his hand in hers, and heard her singing *Amazing Grace*, his favorite verse. His body was suddenly racked with pain, but he didn't care. He felt her warm, sweet breath; her face was touching his. And she was singing softly:

> 'Twas grace that taught my heart to fear,
> And grace my fears reliev'd;
> How precious did that grace appear,
> The hour I first believ'd!

He opened his eyes. He and Hannah were lying on the ground next to the wagon. Hannah May's hand was still on his chest, and when she brought it up to his face, she gently turned it towards hers. Tears of joy poured out of their eyes, as she looked upward to say, "Thank you, Jesus."

Justin was in great pain, dazed and confused. "Jai Krishna," he mumbled.

Hannah May had no idea what he meant and didn't care. She gave thanks again to the good Lord Jesus Christ.

Two years later, the day after Hannah May's eighteenth birthday, Hannah became Mrs. Justin Daniels. It was the biggest wedding the parishioners of the Presbyterian Church had ever seen. Surely the event of the year.

And when the reverend Zachariah said, "Just one more thing before I tie the eternal knot of love between these wonderful young people," he leaned over to Justin and whispered, "Only if you will play and let Hannah sing for us."

Justin nodded, and the Reverend Zack announced loudly, "I now pronounce you man and wife! You may kiss the bride."

The ceremony and the reception were attended by over a hundred people. Once again in front of his flock, the Reverend Zack made an opening announcement.

"Ladies and gentlemen, it is my distinct pleasure to introduce the bride and groom . . . " Justin and Hannah May stepped up onto the platform, and Rev. Zack continued with the surprise, ". . . to sing your favorite hymn."

The crowd cheered like they never could cheer in church. *Amazing Grace* brought tears to the eyes of every adult and even some wild kids who settled down briefly for the rendition.

Zachariah stepped up with his fiddle in hand and said, "Now a couple of the boys and I are gonna kick off this here reception with a song we've never sung in church, *Turkey in the Straw*! But it's okay with the Lord if we sing it out here." He looked up and shouted, "And all God's children said, 'Hallelujah!'" They did, and then the crowd cheered again and the hoedown was under way.

Justin danced round and round with his beaming new wife. And all the men wanted to take a turn dancing with the bride, which Justin didn't mind; he couldn't blame them. So he joined the boys on stage with the new instrument he had picked recently, a conga drum from an island called Madagascar. He'd never heard of the place before but loved playing that drum.

Because Hannah May had inherited a good deal of money from her late father, they had decided to go to the mystical islands called Hawaii on a 150-foot Brigantine called the *Lurline*, owned by a man named Matson, who later formed the world famous Matson Lines. Justin had learned a song written by the Queen of Hawaii, Lilliuokolani. It was very popular in the US and spoke to his heart. It was called *Aloha Oe*. He even picked up a ukulele and taught the song to Hannah May. The title meant, *Until we meet again*. They performed it for everyone at the reception before they left for their honeymoon. Many were a bit envious of the ideal couple, but truly admired and even loved them, and therefore wished them well.

Justin and Hannah May soon had four boys: Matthew, Mark, Luke and John. Justin actually wanted to name one of the boys Krishna. The name had stuck with him after he had found out that Krishna was an Indian God. But Hannah wouldn't have it. Had to be just like in the good book: Matthew, Mark, Luke and John.

After hundreds of conversations about God and the purpose of life, Hannah May and Justin agreed that making others happy was their greatest blessing. Hannah read the Scriptures daily and always felt that they were heaven bound. Justin also read the Bible periodically, becoming fascinated by references to reincarnation. In the Bible it states that John the Baptist had been Elijah in a previous life. Jesus himself was resurrected. So there was something that always lingered in Justin's mind that made him believe that perhaps the end in this life was only the beginning for the next. It didn't really matter one way or the other because their lives were blessed, and they brought happiness to many over the years with their musical talents, wholesome example and sincere willingness to help others. Hannah May and Justin died together in their sleep at the turn of the century.

When the townfolks heard the news, there was not a dry eye anywhere, and a knowing smile graced every face that shared the joy of knowing that sweet couple. Reverend Zack was 90 years old and at the funeral, he offered an inspirational eulogy about the couple everyone loved and admired.

"God bless and God speed these angels to heaven, and since no one will ever sing *Amazing Grace* like

Hannah May again in my lifetime, then I am just going to play *Turkey in the Straw* one last time!" And he proceeded to do exactly that.

This was too much to accept even from the beloved Reverend Zack. Everyone was shocked, unsure what to do or say, but true to his word, it was the last time. He finished with a solemn "Amen" and slowly fell to the ground with a smile on his face, knowing he was going to join his friends Justin and Hannah May. But even with all his great scriptural knowledge from 70 years of preaching, Zack wasn't sure exactly where it would be. When the nearest folks bent over him, the last thing they heard him say in a raspy whisper was, "Time will tell."

He rallied and lifted his head a little bit to say, "... See you in church!"

And then there was just one more Sunday-morning, winning smile on his lips, and he was gone, perhaps to heaven . . . or on another mission for God.

Chapter Seven

Gabriel

San Antonio, Texas USA

Born in 1910 in San Antonio, Texas, Gabriel Jose was deeply loved by his mother, Antoinette, from Paducah, Kentucky. Of French decent, Antoinette left home when she was 18. Gabe was born on the 15th of November two years later on an unusually humid day. It was no accident that he was given the name Gabriel on that day, because Antoinette knew well that the book of Revelations 11:15 says that when the Angel Gabriel blows his horn, it will be announcing Judgment Day.

Antoinette thought Gabriel deserved an Archangel's name, especially since she was reading scripture that morning before she went into labor. Gabriel's father, Ramiero Mateo, was ecstatic when the child arrived in their little one room shack. Antoinette's dearest friend, Magdalena, coached Antoinette through the birth, but as the baby's head began to crown, she said, "Ramiero, por favor." She stood back and let Ramiero hold the baby's wet and blood-covered head. As it slid into his hands, he gently turned the baby over, and Gabriel opened his eyes and smiled.

Ramiero laughed and cried, and although he carefully pulled Gabriel out, he had to let Magdalena take it from there to cut the umbilical cord, as he felt weak as a kitten and happier than he had ever been. Gabe and Ramiero bonded forever in those priceless moments.

Ramiero loved his precious Antoinette and worshiped little Gabriel, their only child, and worked incredibly long, arduous hours as a wrangler. When Gabriel was old enough to go to a little local school, Antoinette began working at a canning factory two miles from their home.

The prejudice against Mexicans at that time in history, especially in Texas, was all too common even though the Mexican American War was long over. Bigotry is an evil trait that lingers like a sickness for whatever reason and always brings out the worst in the human animal.

Ramiero and Antoinette lived on the outskirts of the cowboy town of San Antonio. The folks who knew them, loved them and could overlook the fact that she had creamy, white skin, and he was dark and burly. Many white men called him "big and ugly." Ramiero was not afraid of any man, but he was smart enough to bite his tongue and back off when any trouble arose. Sometimes groups of locals would yell, "Hey, big and ugly!" They all thought that was hilarious, but not one would ever have said that to him face to face. Even though he had a Spanish name, he was born in Texas and was married to a white woman.

From his birth until his early twenties, Gabe was deeply loved. He never minded the hardships of the Depression; he never really thought of it. Beans and rice were his favorite meal; homemade tortillas were a special treat. There was something about food cooked in lard that didn't agree with him. Antoinette knew it and favored a diet with as many vegetables and fruits as they could get; meat just didn't appeal to him, which was good from an economic point of view. They did have chickens, and Gabe did eat eggs. Gabriel was also a natural gardener; he loved it and seemed to care more for such things than any of his peers.

He had no qualms about saying he was always glad that he was not brought up in snow country, even though he had never been north of San Antonio. Although there were some cold days in the winter that chilled him, in the long run it was still Texas. There was always a fire in the wood stove when it was cold, and summer always came sooner or later. Sometimes at night he had dreams of living in a round-shaped home made out of ice and stinking of dead fish. And in the dream, when he would go outside, there was a bitterly cold blizzard, sometimes a complete white out. He would wake up shivering from the cold even though it was a dream. Antoinette or Ramiero were always there to comfort him and warm him up.

He was a teenager before he ever heard of the North Pole or knew such a place existed. It sent chills down his spine each time he thought of it. He was so grateful he did not live in such a place.

"Gracias a Dios!" (Thank you, God!) he would say out loud. Often he would think to himself, *I will never live in a frozen ice house like that,* and then he heard a voice in his head that said, "Never again," which confused him, but seemed acceptable.

He wasn't talking to himself and knew it because Antoinette told him that the other voice in his head was God. When he asked about the devil she would say, "He is not allowed in your head Gabriel--and if you ever hear him, tell him, 'Git out, Diablo, adios.'"

Of course, Gabriel Jose became fluent in Spanish and English, but his mother spoke to him in English most of the time. She would say "Gabriel, please speak English; after all, we are Texans." And Gabe liked nothing better than pleasing his petite, ever sweet mother. He was proud to be a Texan.

At twelve years of age, Gabriel was given an old, beat up Spanish guitar by his mother and father for Christmas. He thought it was the most wonderful gift he would ever receive from anyone in his life.

Antoinette insisted that he learn a song for the church picnic. He balked but finally gave in. The song was *When the Saints Go Marching in,* and he realized when he heard all the verses why she wanted him to learn it.

> *"And when Gabriel blows his horn,*
> *when Gabriel blows his horn,*
> *Lord, let me be in that number*
> *when Gabriel blows his horn."*

Gabriel never blew a horn, but he took to the guitar like he'd been playing it forever. He played every day. A friend of his father's named Juan Di Dios Fernando A. was a flamenco guitar player and dancer. He recognized an intense natural talent for the guitar and a similar inclination for rhythm and dancing in Gabriel and happily spent the next few years teaching and working with his protégé, Gabriel Jose.

There was jealousy among the other boys as Gabriel was so talented, dark like his father but very good looking like his mother. Most peers could not help but like him; he was the most generous of the boys, not only in giving flowers to the girls but part of his lunch to another boy or marbles to younger kids. He was simply good-natured. He had not a negative bone in his body except that it was difficult for him to be tolerant when there were prejudicial remarks about him. But he bit his lip and managed. By the time he was twenty, he had filled out like his dad, Ramiero, who was six-foot-four. At five-foot ten-inches tall, Gabe was nearly as wide in the shoulders. But, as opposed to Ramiero, nobody could call him ugly; he was simply too handsome by any standard. He was a man's man but with a sweet nature more like a woman, his father thought, but not in a negative sense.

Gabriel dated several girls, and enjoyed their company, as would any young man. He played soccer and other rugged sports with his amigos. He differed from the others because of the time he spent in the garden. And he often sought solace in the nearby woods where he would practice his guitar and sing many songs. His favorite was a traditional Mexican folk song entitled *Por Un Amor*. Because of Juan Di Dios Fernando A., he also became an expert on the classic Spanish instrumental *Malagueña*.

This serious time alone in the woods led him frequently into setting the guitar down and deep introspection, sitting erect with his legs crossed and his eyes closed. It was at these times that Gabriel would have amazing visions that he felt he could not explain to anyone.

They were never exactly the same but sometimes similar. His favorite was more like a daydream of being on a beach with black sand, palm trees, and soft, warm breezes. He knew it was not Texas or Mexico, for there could not be such a thing as black sand. In the vision a marvelously beautiful Mexican woman wearing a skirt of grass and no top was walking slowly towards him with some kind of large, flowered necklace draped around her shoulders and flowing over her full breasts. She was like no other woman he had ever seen in real life, and she was singing with an angelic voice in a language he did not recognize.

It made no sense to him, but he couldn't forget it. He felt that the woman in the dream would finally become his wife someday. But he knew it was just another daydream. He had heard the term "soulmate," but didn't know for sure if people lived more than one life.

Automobiles were primitive in the twenties and thirties. Boys all liked seeing photos of cars and seeing them in the movies at the Majestic Theater. Gabriel's favorite was a bright red, 1932 Ford Deuce Roadster. But he had a vision that he could not understand in which he was driving some kind of car of the future, he presumed. How could he know that it was a 1965 Pontiac GTO? It was only

1933; such things were not to be for many years. He didn't know what it meant, only that he was in the vehicle driving, and there were many other brightly colored, super modern vehicles on a busy highway with hundreds of cars, different shapes and sizes like he had never seen before. And the woman with him each time was the exotic beauty from the black sand beach with long, black hair waving in the wind. There was also a big puppy sitting in the back seat with ears standing up in the wind. It was an uncanny dream.

Gabriel's family didn't own a car when he was young; he had never even driven a real automobile, only an old wagon pulled by his father's work horse. The automobile vision always left him excited and confused.

Late one afternoon near dusk, he had fallen into a gentle state of stillness leaning against a pine tree, eyes closed and almost sleeping, yet awake and at peace. He felt a soft, wet tongue on the back of his hand. He thought it was the puppy from the convertible, but he was awake. The long, wet tongue licked gently on his forearm and then back on the top of his hand. It was no daydream, he thought, as he slowly opened his eyes. It was a large, dirty dog, which smelled foul, but looked up with eyes that penetrated Gabriel's. He remembered the time his priest had told him, "God sees us through the eyes of animals." He rarely went to Mass, but he remembered the comment, and in looking into the animal's eyes, he found himself and the dog almost hypnotized for a few minutes.

Finally, Gabe moved slightly, and the dog backed off, a bit skittish. The dog looked famished. Probably scary to some people, he had a large frame, with medium length splotches of grey and black hair. It took a moment for Gabriel to realize that the animal was probably thirsty, so he quickly pulled out his water bag and poured some in his hand. The animal rapidly lapped it up. Gabe poured more until it was all gone. The penetrating look passed between them again a few times. They were old, old friends. Gabriel noticed a leather collar around the dog's neck.

It was loose probably because the dog had not eaten in a while. He removed it to get a better look. It was a wide collar, probably to secure such a big animal. On the opposite side from the buckle, a name was burned in bold letters: KARMA.

Gabriel smiled his winning smile as he spoke softly, "Hola, Señor Karma."

He thought the dog smiled back. In time, he would know that Karma truly was smiling at him.

"Good boy, Karma, good Karma!"

He put the collar back on Karma a notch tighter, and jumped to his feet.

"Karma, are you hungry? Come on, boy, let's go meet my mama; she will fix you a little perro fiesta."

Gabriel had fallen in love with Karma, as did his parents, but with some hesitation at first. Karma was a huge dog. And they did not know him. Gabe knew instinctively that Karma was to be his best friend for many years, but nevertheless, he set out to find the owners in every way he could. He posted signs in town and around the village. He asked everyone he knew. Old friends from school met and loved Karma, and as time moved forward, Karma regained his health, due to the food that Antoinette brought home from the cannery and the meat that Gabriel didn't eat. Karma grew strong, but always as gentle as a kitten according to Antoinette. He didn't even chase the chickens, and when other dogs would try, Karma would chase them off, obviously considering it his job to protect the family's chickens. For a reward, he received fried eggs with his beans and rice every morning, like the rest of the family.

Often Karma would accompany Ramiero to his job. Ramiero would take his horse, Antonio, and gallop two miles with Karma right beside him. It gave Karma a great workout, and when they had to slow down through the village, none of the local bigots even thought about calling Ramiero, "ugly," because they quickly realized that Karma knew what they were thinking, and a deep growl let them know they were making a mistake.

Nobody ever claimed to own Karma, but not because Gabe didn't try to get the word out.

At one point, Gabriel went to the old San Antonio library and tried to research the name *Karma*. It set him off on a reading journey that was enlightening indeed for his inquisitive, young mind. He soon found out that Karma was not a name, but a condition of life. He didn't know a thing about India or a religion called Hinduism. Indians to him were the Mescalero-Apaches and the Comanches who had struck fear in the early Texans but sadly became a conquered lot seen around bars and alleys in town. They were proud Native Americans who had been taken down by alcohol, and being aware of that gave Gabriel reason not to drink. Plus the fact that Juan Di Dios Fernando A. had told him, "Gabriel, if you ever start drinking liquor, I will never teach you another guitar lick."

As Gabriel began to study what *karma* meant and the information that was available about the country of India and their deities like Buddha and Krishna, it began to be life changing for him. He had been raised Catholic like his mother and father, but this new information about the meaning of karma brought him into contact with the idea of meditation. As he read more about meditation, he hungered for still more information about it and, therefore, rather removed himself from any post high school social crowds while he studied the practice of meditation.

Germany attacked Poland on September 1, 1939, and the world changed. It became smaller. Cowboys and locals at bars in Texas talked about "the war, and the S.O.B. Hitler."

Americans were beginning to get angry at the dictator known as the Fuhrer. Gabriel was a well respected gardener and a local entertainer who performed in and around San Antonio area most of the time. He had enjoyed the company of many lovely women and graciously so, but had never found the woman on the black sand beach he had dreamt of, although he kept searching for her, heart and soul.

It was estimated that Karma was about two years old when he came to Gabe. Now he weighed over 90 pounds and still ran with Ramiero every day he could. And when Gabriel had performances, Karma would be right on stage beside him. Gabe would introduce Karma every time he performed, but in time it was not necessary. As soon as he would say, "Hola; I want to introduce my best friend," the crowd would start chanting, "Karma, Karma, Karma."

Having learned what Karma meant, Gabriel just figured it was a good chant for anyone. He would smile and open his act with *Malagueña*. Karma would sit comfortably beside him like a monolithic animal god.

The performances were enthralling for all, especially Gabriel, his mom and dad and Juan Di Dios Fernandos A.

By this time Gabriel had researched enough on Buddha to be able to purposely go into a silent meditation and find deep peace within, always with Karma close by. In his daily life, he longed for the woman of his dreams. Karma and Gabe would still spend their time in the woods together, practicing guitar and new songs, dreaming and meditating.

When money finally permitted, Gabe moved away from his parents' home and into a small house near downtown San Antonio. Eventually, Juan Di Dios began acting as a manager and agent, booking Gabe in honky-tonks, pubs, bars, and other small venues within driving distance of "San Antone." Naturally, there were always women who flocked to see Gabriel; he was always a crowd pleaser.

But the drunken audiences were generally not so impressed with "Old Mexican music." Even though Gabe was young and vibrant, the crowds in the bars were generally older and inebriated, and more ready for western swing and the likes of Bob Willes and the Texas Cowboys or Al Dexter with songs like "Honky Tonk Blues."

It didn't bother Gabe; he enjoyed performing his material and his unique style. Given a chance, he usually quieted rowdy audiences and touched a mellow side of the folks he would entertain. No matter what, he had a following and his ever faithful Karma.

In his research on karma he found a quote by an Indian man named Mahatma Gandhi. It stuck with him as he was searching for the right thing to do spiritually in his life: "Self-indulgence leads to destruction, and renunciation to immortality."

Gabe tried to understand what renunciation meant; he had thought for a time about the priesthood, which was his only other exposure to the term. He was soon to realize, however, that something else so wonderful was coming his way that being a monk would not be his destiny in this life. Soon he would meet "Angel."

After finally retiring one night after dealing with a particularly obnoxious crowd at a bar called the Drag-On-Inn, he experienced a nightmare where he was in pain, lying on the deck of a filthy, oceangoing vessel in a torrential downpour. There were other men trying to cling to the slippery deck who looked emaciated, and thirty feet away from them in a makeshift pen, there were countless, agonized pigs, squealing relentlessly. He was slipping around on the deck as the ship pitched back and forth at such a rate as to make him slide even more. Then it rocked steeply to the starboard side, a huge wave smashed into the deck, and he was washed into the violent sea. He woke up soaking wet, in a cold sweat. He immediately rolled over and called, "Karma . . . Karma, Karma." He reached out, and felt the huge head of his companion next to his small bed.

"Thank God for you, Karma. Good Karma; good boy."

Karma's ears stood up and forward when Gabe scratched behind them. Gabe never knew it, but Karma was half German Shepherd, mixed with a then rare breed in the US called Akitas from Japan, originally bred to work in pairs and quarter bears for hunters.

The dream happened a couple of times. Gabe was glad that he never ate pork and was a strict vegetarian. He craved his Texas vegetables and fruits. He was a rare, sober, introspective young man, who had become a vegetarian of his own volition. He was the only one he knew. Whenever he was served meat, it somehow wound up in

Karma's mouth. Over time he had given up most meat but still ate eggs and cheese.

In studying Hinduism Gabriel learned that the word *Om* meant *God* and was a sacred chant. He read about a god named Krishna. Although he had never heard the name before, when he read it, he closed his eyes and repeated softly what the book mentioned to do in worship of the God Krishna, "Jai Krishna, Jai Krishna, Jai Krishna."

Gabe knew he should be saying, "Praise Jesus," but felt that "Jai Krishna" was okay, too. When he did a little more research, he discovered that *Jai* meant *victory*, and the phrase *Jai Krishna* implied that if the Lord Krishna was successful in teaching devotees (followers) to go within and meditate deeply, they would reach a more Godly state of mind, understanding the God within. Therefore, Lord Krishna would be victorious in his mission to uplift those seekers who followed the precepts of the teachings of the Bhagavad Gita (the Hindu holy book).

Nobody had ever mentioned anything like this in Gabe's Catholic upbringing, but *Jai Krishna* sounded so very familiar, even though he had never heard the phrase in his life.

He read more and decided to study more about exactly how to meditate, not just the personal style he had fashioned. He thought that since he could not find a woman who was right for him, perhaps he should be a monk or a priest. But he also craved a soul mate and a family.

He was keeping his doors open, pursuing his singing career and enjoying his life. He was a proud and loyal American and even thought about joining the army, although he had no desire to be a soldier, even though one time he had a dream of being a Revolutionary soldier. It seemed so real; he was an officer, and he died in battle. Gabe knew he would never really want to be a soldier and would go only if called, and he had to defend his country.

While visiting the local mercantile store in town inquiring about zucchini seeds for his garden, his life was suddenly changed. He saw a woman of such extraordinary beauty that he was dumbfounded. She was his height with long, black, shiny hair. She was wearing a gingham dress, which could not hide her shapely body, and nothing could compare to her extraordinary smile. She was dark skinned, but he thought she could not be of Mexican heritage. She looked different for some reason, more than anything a lot like the island beauty of his dreams. She was the very woman that he had dreamed of, and she was standing there right in front of him, like a perfectly sculpted Italian marble statue. She stepped up to him and said something in a language he didn't recognize, and leaned down beside him, bumping his arm with her breast by accident. He gulped and looked down as she petted Karma. Karma was also enchanted.

She looked up with a shy expression and said, "Mexican-Sei Messicano?" (Are you a Mexican?)

He clearly understood her question. "No . . . Habla español?"

"No," she said, with her face a few inches from Gabe's. The breathing was heavy for both of them.

She smiled another soft smile and said, "Io sono de Pisa, Italia." (I am from Pisa, Italy.)

He was at his wit's end, when a voice behind him said, "She said she is from Italy, a town called Pisa."

Italian marble statue? Gabe thought. He turned to see a heavy man, perhaps older than he, with a pleasant expression on his face.

Gabriel inquired kindly, "How do you know this woman?"

"I am Mario; let me introduce my sister, Francesca."

Gabe turned to her and said, "Hola, Francesca!"

She returned the smile and said, "Hola, yourself, Señor Gabriel!"

Now he was really confused.

Mario and Francesca laughed at their inside joke. "You speak English, Francesca?"

"Yes, Gabriel, English, French, Portuguese, and Italian, and a little bit of Spanish as well. You never noticed me, but I have been at some of your performances, and I think you are a wonderful musician, and "Tu sei affiscinante." (You are handsome.)

The only woman with a perfect clef chin and dimples that Gabriel had ever seen in his life was this island girl from his dreams. Now this angelic embodiment of that dream was right there in front of him. And she put him in heaven with her presence. She kept winking with her left eye as if she was trying to tell him something. Every once in a while, she would stop and hold her hand over her left eye. Before long she said, "Please excuse me, I have a twitch in my eye when I get nervous or excited."

Gabriel spoke softly, leaning closer to the beauty and taking on his irresistible charm. "Are you nervous or excited?"

She leaned even closer and said in a whisper as though Mario would not hear, "Both, mi amigo."

The three of them got along famously; Mario was a great humorist. Gabriel and Francesca enjoyed his stories immensely but could never take their eyes off each other. Karma was a little confused. He sat on the floor between their stools in the cafe looking back and forth. He had never seen Gabe pay attention to anyone to the point where he didn't look at Karma at least every once in a while.

He whined softly, and Gabe said, "Shhhhh, Karma," as he motioned downward with his hand, still not looking at anything but the riveting eyes of Francesca. Karma lay down obediently, looking up and then putting his head between his front legs and shutting his eyes.

By the time Gabriel had remembered that he had been in the mercantile store to get seeds, they had been sitting at the San Antone Cafe for an hour.

Gabe looked at his watch, a proud possession Juan Di Dios had given him so he could keep track of the time he spent on each set when he was performing. He knew he had to get ready for a show and invited Mario and Francesca to come and see him perform.

"We were planning on it, Gabriel," said Mario. When they just sat there staring at each other, Mario continued, "You look like Johnny Weismiller in *Tarzan of the Apes* . . . when he saw the first woman in his life." He paused, feeling ignored. Gabe smiled at Francesca, finally turned his head slightly towards Mario, and said, "Gracias." He obviously hadn't heard a word Mario said.

"Love at first sight," Mario said. "Tarzan never looked at a monkey that way."

Neither one of them heard him. It was like two soul mates who had been searching life after life to find each other. Little did they know, that was exactly what was happening.

Mario and Francesca became regulars at Gabe's performances. She worked at the Majestic Theater in downtown San Antonio and was able to get tickets on the nights when Gabe didn't have performances and was in town. Needless to say, everybody adored Francesca. Mario was always charming but very protective of his little sister. He was ten years older. Mario and Francesca were brought from "the old country" (Italy) to the US when Mario was eleven and Francesca was still a baby. When Francesca was ten years old, their parents met an unfortunate demise when their train was derailed on the way to San Antonio to pick up their kids, where they were staying with relatives. They were comforted in their grief by relatives and the priest of the church on the other end of San Antonio and raised as Catholics.

Gabriel was amazed that in all their years in the same town, he had never seen her. And that she had seen him perform, but he never noticed her. When they finally did meet, he could never forget her. Mario, who had been her stalwart and serious guardian knew the minute the two met that he was off duty. Deep down he was relieved and grateful. He loved his little sister beyond belief; he just felt such great confidence in Gabe that he was able to let down his guard more than ever before. Mario and Francesca lived together, but they both knew it was past time for them to have their own places.

It was a fairy book romance. As townspeople began to know Gabe had found his true love, many men in the town were put off because they never had a chance to even meet the Italian beauty known to a close few as "Cheska."

Men always had their eyes on "Cheska," no matter where she went. Many of the men who watched Gabe grow up and date all the most popular girls were jealous of the rising, young star. It seemed he had everything. There was even a little jealousy on Karma's part at first, but soon Karma had taken on the role of being loyal and protective to both Gabriel and Cheska. Although he was a large dog with a husky build, his temperament was like a puppy. He never growled, unless he had to let another dog know it would be unwise to get into it with him.

San Antonio is on the edge of a humid, subtropical climate zone and is relatively warm year-round. Gabe always loved the warm weather. Cheska and Gabe walked for hours in the countryside. He had always felt blessed that he didn't live in a freezing cold climate. One of his bad dreams of being in a bitterly cold environment featured him carrying a dead buck over his shoulders in knee deep snow, his legs and feet totally numb.

In another dream of being so cold, he was indoors in a freezing room somewhere, putting his feet inside a woman's parka up against her bare breasts. He remembered how warm it felt, but the dream was so absurd he never told anyone. In fact, he rarely talked about his dreams, either the good ones or those that appeared totally absurd, as dreams seem to be to most people who don't comprehend that they might be memories of the past, or even more preposterous, possibly visions of the future.

One dream was more like a nightmare, in which he found himself on a freezing ice surface with Karma looking up at him with copious amounts of blood pouring out of his mouth. Gabe shook his head and turned over, and the vision persisted, but it wasn't Karma, it was some kind of wolf. He remembered crying and asking the animal for forgiveness.

He did tell Cheska about the dream, and as always, she would say, "It's just a bad dream Gabe, it will pass. Karma is okay." That was the reassurance he needed. And it seemed that whatever came up in a negative light, she always had a comforting comment. And always with the incomparable smile of an angel. She was too good to be true for Gabe.

Of course, Gabe told her how Karma originally came to him in the woods, that they bonded instantly, and how he had searched for the owners but could never find them. He also explained what karma meant as far as Buddhist and Hindu teachings. Cheska was very intelligent and well-read. Her mother had tried to give her an overview of several world religions when she was young, and although she was Catholic, like Gabriel she enjoyed learning about other religions.

Cheska told Gabe, "I love the concept of karma; so did my mother. She said that it made so much sense that if you try to do good, and help others, the rewards will be that the good things in life come back to you."

Gabe said, "It's in the Bible, too: 'Do onto others as you would have others do unto you.'"

"But with karma, it means not just in this life, it means in the next life, too," Cheska said softly. They silently agreed.

They looked at each other, deep into the subtle glowing eyes of true love. It was a moment in time they felt had happened many times before. They simply sat there. They both sensed the silver thread of life that had been weaving for many lifetimes, "many incarnations," said Cheska ever so softly.

And then, as if answering the question she was posing, "Soul mates must be, uh . . . reincarnated together sometimes."

"Will you marry me, Francesca?"

Her left eye twitched a few times; she put her delicate hand over it for a moment, grinned, and asked, "Have you been married before?"

"No," he said sitting up straight, "at least not in this life."

She smiled again. "Maybe to me a hundred years ago?"

They embraced one another and kissed a long, deep kiss that led them to deeper and deeper passion, standing in the warm light of the sunset. Karma, who was always nearby, watched for a few minutes, did not understand the boring scenario he had seen before, but knew it might take a while. He found some cool grass in the shade of an oak tree and went to sleep.

That evening after a particularly rowdy audience with the drunkards at the Drag-On-Inn, Cheska, Gabe and Mario were walking back to Mario's old Ford. They were discussing the fact that all of them had had enough of these kinds of gigs. And then Gabriel stopped, put his arm around Cheska, turned, and looked Mario in the face.

"Mario, I would like to ask you for Cheska's hand in marriage."

"Gabriel, why are you are asking me?"

"Because it's the right thing to do, and . . . I want you to be my best man."

"I am honored."

"Why do you feel you want me to give you permission?"

"Because you love Cheska, and your father is no longer here, and . . . and, well, I don't know how to say it, but . . ."

"Please, Gabe, speak up."

"You are the only one with a car, and we need to go to Mexico to get married."

They all laughed. Mario laughed the loudest and the longest as they all continued to stroll toward Mario's 1936 Ford Coupe about 200 feet away.

And then they heard a familiar, obnoxious voice behind them. It was Sammy, one of the young town drunks who grew up with Gabe and always resented his good looks and popularity. He was with three others who had been at the same table, throwing down shots of whisky and beer chasers all night. And making stupid remarks, of course. They were pretty drunk.

"Ya'll Mexicans hang out together like rats in a trap, don't ya?" Sammy said.

Mario picked up the pace, and Gabe and Cheska followed suit. Evidently Sammy had taken it upon himself to be the spokesperson of the motley crew, while the others egged him on. Even though Sammy had known Gabe since they were kids and was well aware that Gabe was born in Texas, he had deep resentment and jealousy coming to the surface.

"How come you Mexican dudes are so ugly? You are as ugly as your old man, but the Mexican señorita bitch is sooooo fine."

Gabe stopped in his path and turned to face them.

Mario wheeled around to Gabe and said, "Let's get out of here."

"Yes," said Francesca; "Let's go!"

Before they could do anything else, the four drunks were circled around them. Sammy stepped forward, wavering a little, reached out and put his hand flat on Francesca's chest, freely feeling her firm breasts. She stepped back, disgusted. Gabe had never been in a fight, nor had Mario, who was big, but overweight and out of shape. The four guys around them were all scrappers. Nevertheless Gabe unleashed a furious punch in Sammy's face, breaking his nose. Sammy was too inebriated even to feel it. He started fighting back, with two of his chums also teaming up on Gabe, whose adrenalin was giving him uncommon strength on top of his innate muscularity. The fourth guy had targeted Mario and was pummeling his stomach mercilessly with boxing punches. It didn't take long before the two thugs had Gabe pulled back by his arms. Gabe was angry and tired, and the attackers were all aggressively drunk to the point of violence. Sammy's nose was bleeding profusely. "Ya'll did this to me, you shit!"

He wiped the blood with his sleeve and hand and stepped over, grabbing Cheska again and with his other hand, he smeared the blood on her neck, chest and dress, laughing like a hyena.

"Do you even believe in God, you heathens?" Cheska screamed.

Gabe's neck had been twisted and his head was bent over, but he painfully lifted it up and spoke softly to the bully, "Do you believe in KARMA?"

Laughing loudly, "Do you mean your dog?"

At that point Karma drove his nose right into Sammy's groin with his mouth wide open and a deep, guttural growling that sent shivers down the spines of the other three jerks. They immediately dropped Gabe's arms and ran, as did the guy who had beat big Mario to the ground.

It was all Gabe could do to pull the 95-pound animal off Sammy, who was screaming in agony, as Karma had torn through his Levis and ripped open his leg. It was hard to tell how bad the bite was, but it looked like more than one gash around his groin and thighs.

Gabe stared at the blood dripping from Karma's mouth and flashed back on the nightmare with Karma's bloody mouth dripping in the snow. He blinked his eyes and shook his head, got on his knees and wrapped his arm around Karma's neck, hugging him and pulling him off Sammy. Then he stood up; Cheska and Gabe hugged each other for a minute and began helping Mario stand up. He was bent over for several minutes. He groaned, "We'd best get Sammy a doctor." Sammy was moaning in agony, begging for help.

Gabe calmly leaned down to Sam and said, "There are two kinds of karma, good karma and bad karma. Now you know what bad karma is, don't ever touch my woman again, and don't ever come near any of us or I can promise . . . more bad karma!"

Karma had calmed down and was sitting there breathing hard. He had not had this much fun in a couple of years and was thinking of how great he used to feel after running for miles with Ramiero galloping to the corral and back, dog endorphins.

When Mario and Gabe finally dragged Sammy to the car, Karma growled all the way. Once they sat him up in the back seat, Gabe was on one side and Karma was on the other. There was a low guttural sound every time Karma looked in Sammy's direction. Gabe leaned towards Sammy and whispered, "Sammy, just say, 'Good Karma,' and that will mellow him out."

Sammy moaned in pain and in a crackling voice stuttered, "GGGGood Karma."

Karma bared his teeth and growled viciously as Sammy, filled with fright, leaned against the window of the old Ford coupe. "I guess you don't deserve good karma yet," said Cheska. And then, with a glance at the fear in Sammy's face, her deep, loving side surfaced as she put her hand gently on Karma's muzzle and said, "It's okay Karma, no more growling. Sammy is sorry and he has had enough." Then in all sincerity she touched Sammy's shoulder and said, "I know you are in pain, Sammy, and we'll get you to a doctor soon." She smiled a comforting smile, and Sammy let out a sigh of sorrow, and the pain eased a bit as though he had been touched by an angel, which he had.

Unfortunately the only doctor they could find was a veterinarian who knew Karma and loved him, but he also happened to know Sammy's family and what a dangerous drunk Sammy could be. He told Gabe that he thought he would be all right and he would take him home after he patched him up.

Early the next morning, Cheska made the decision that the time was right to head for Matamoras, Mexico. Cheska had been dreaming of being Mrs. Gabriel Jose Mateo. And Gabe was in heaven, even if his neck was a little sore. Mario was in considerable pain from the battering he had received but said nothing. It was to be a glorious day.

Following close behind Mario's ford, Antoinette was in seventh heaven with the thought of her Angel Gabriel marrying the divine Cheska, as was Ramiero, who was driving his Chevy pickup truck. Karma had jumped in the back for a change and was enjoying the wind in his face, remembering how much fun he had the night before.

As they cruised south of the border, Gabe was singing "Por un Amor" to Cheska, Mario casually asked, "I've got nothing against Mexicans, but why didn't you tell them we were Italians and not Mexicans last night?"

Gabe thought about it for a minute and said, "When they started beating us up and manhandling Cheska, I thought about it. But I don't think we had their attention until they met Karma!"

The vows were short and simple, and the wedding day could not have been better. Back home again, where they had their reception with about a hundred friends and neighbors standing around and clapping, the bride and groom kissed and secured their future forever, once again.

Following their honeymoon in Austin a few days later, Cheska and Gabe were hooked on the sweet, little town. Before long they had made the move.

Mario soon met a woman, a delightful woman his age named Britney in San Antonio and moved in with her. They shared much in common. He was pleased that Cheska was with Gabe and began taking care of his own life, having been officially relieved of his self-imposed guardianship duty.

As it turned out, Cheska, unbeknownst to her, was a natural singer. She had learned an old song called *Amazing Grace* in church, and Gabe heard her singing it one evening in their bungalow. He began backing her up, and in no time, inviting her on stage. From that point on she was always an audience pleaser. At one such gig when Cheska stepped up to the stage beside Gabe's chair, she began singing *Amazing Grace*. With the back light behind her head, there was a glow. Gabe was in awe; he blinked his eyes, and she appeared to have long, blond, curly hair flowing over her shoulders and . . . a glowing halo. He shook his head and blinked again. He could see a stained glass window behind her. His heart skipped a beat. He closed his eyes, thinking how great his karma was to have such an angel.

The song was over before the vision dissipated. But the vision was indelible. He called Cheska, "Angel," on stage that night, and it stuck with the fans. They began to be known as Angel and Gabe. And soon there were two new members in the group who both played fiddle, banjo and guitar. Juan coined the marketing ploy of calling them *Angel and Gabe and the Heavenly Host*. Sometimes Gabe would play a Cuban conga drum that felt as natural to him as his guitar. He occasionally had dreams and visions of playing a shell drum somewhere in what he thought was a grass shack; the visions were short, but joyful, as opposed to his dream about the "Pig boat," which he eventually explained to Cheska. The story so affected her that she, too, refused to eat pork and quickly became a vegetarian.

Gabe was so good on the Conga, and had such a dazzling Latin look, that some compared him to a young Cuban singer and conga player named Desi Arnaz, the very same Desi Arnaz who had his own orchestra and eventually joined forces with a lovely, red-headed actress named Esmeralda McGillicuddy, one day to be known to all the world as Lucille Ball.

Time and again, fans would tell Angel and Gabe that they were better looking and more talented than Lucy and Desi. They were too modest to do anything but smile sincerely and blush. Although they became quite successful in Austin, San Antonio, and other towns in central Texas, they were satisfied with their careers. Cheska graduated from the University of Austin, and Gabe pursued his gardening vocation and received a degree in horticulture.

With the birth of their daughter, Angelica, they were on cloud nine. They had purchased a bungalow in Austin, and Mario bought the house they had in San Antonio.

Karma was little older, but still a formidable animal and ever faithful to Gabe and Cheska. When Angelica came along, he had a new unconditional love. God have mercy on anyone who might even consider harming that child. It was just understood that when Karma was with "Angie," only a few, other than Cheska and Gabe, could get near her without hearing a long, low growl: Mario, Britney, Juan Di Dios, and, of course, the proud grandparents, Ramiero and Antoinette.

Cheska had a lifelong fear of trains and refused to ride on them. This was not unusual considering both her parents died in a horrendous train accident when she was only ten. The phobia was never talked about; she just refused to ride on trains.

Juan Di Dios had booked Angel and Gabe and the Heavenly Host in New Orleans for a well-paying gig that would last two weeks. But when it was finally confirmed, they had only a day to get there. Not only did Gabe and Cheska not want to leave Angie, but the train was the only option. Of course, Antoinette gladly volunteered to stay at their home and take care of the baby. Juan swore they would never get another opportunity like this one. A record producer from Muscle Shoals was coming just to hear them. And the remuneration from the club was the best offer they had ever had. They had very little savings and could not afford to miss the opportunity.

They were scheduled to catch the old Texas Eagle at 8:00 pm on November 15, Gabe's birthday, from the Sunset Station, built in 1902. It had been a blustery winter day, and Gabe's mother felt intuitively that they should cancel. Since Gabe's birth, she felt he would die on his birthday, because for some reason, God would need his Archangel Gabriel to blow the horn. And in Antoinette's mind it would be the end of time for her. It was a convoluted vision and she knew it, but she had never been able to shake the thought.

The decision was made. As they boarded the classic steam engine, Mario was there with Antoinette and Karma. Karma wanted to come along, but Gabe told him, "No." Karma still tried to board the train. The porter tried to stop him but learned quickly that Karma could be persuasive with nothing more than a deep, foreboding growl. Gabe stood on the step as the train began to pull away to make sure Karma couldn't get on.

But Karma began running beside the train. As Gabe said, "Get back, Karma, stay," he went up the steps to the top of the steel catwalk flooring on the last passenger car. He turned to tell Karma one more time, but Karma made an enormous leap, landing his two front legs on the second step of the catwalk with his rear legs hanging off, flailing for something to step onto. The train was going relatively fast now, and the conductor had to climb over Gabe to run forward several cars to try and make the engineer stop.

Meanwhile, Gabe had gone down on his knees on the top step with his legs hooked under the deck and managed to grab Karma by his front legs, just below the shoulders. He pulled hard, and Karma howled in pain, his rear legs being dragged and torn up on the gravel and railroad ties beneath the car. Cheska laid down on the deck and wrapped her arms around Gabe's waist, clinging to him desperately. The train was going forty-two miles an hour now and gaining speed. Gabe's naturally superior shoulder muscles and healthy biceps were pulling as hard as possible. Cheska screamed, "Save Karma, Gabe!"

In one quick move, grabbing Karma around his massive chest, Gabe exerted a final effort, jerking himself into an upright position and holding Karma tight to his body. Cheska had the same kind of diehard embrace around Gabe's chest. The three were balanced precariously on the steps but, safe from falling, they held each other tight as the train screamed down the fifty-year old-tracks across the Texas flatland at 70 miles an hour.

Eventually the conductor made it back, and with the help of some cowboys in the box car, they started pulling Gabe, Cheska and Karma in as one tight unit; first Cheska, who fought to not let go, but had to, then Gabe, who wouldn't let go of Karma and held him tight because the amazing, bloodied animal was exhausted and growling at everyone except Gabe and Cheska.

Once they were in the passenger car, onlookers gathered near, and a pullman waiter brought Gabe and Cheska blankets, towels and water. They sat on the floor on each side of Karma, petting him and comforting him. His rear legs and paws were bloody and caked with gravel and dirt. After a while, the conductor said, "Mr. Mateo . . ."

Gabe looked up, still holding Karma's head in his lap. "We are stopping the train and will have to put the dog off."

Gabe gave him a serious look.

The intimidated conductor paused, putting his hand to his chin as if to consider options, looked at Karma and said, without much authority, "Well, uh, we will definitely have to put the dog off at the next station."

Gabe responded with a smile of absolute confidence.
"I don't think so, pal; he stays with us. Unless you want to try to move him."

The crowd applauded. And for some unknown reason, Cheska, who was rarely spontaneous, began to sing *Amazing Grace*. By then the rest of the group was there, and the crowd could hear the incomparable voice of Cheska with harmony from the "Heavenly Host."

The Texas Eagle picked up speed again and roared on to New Orleans. The folks on that trip would never forget the astounding scenario with Karma, Gabe, Angel, and the Heavenly Host; many of them promised to be at the upcoming gig.

Karma lay comfortably with his head still in Gabe's lap, dreaming of how much fun it was chomping on Sammy's leg.

It was not surprising that Juan Di Dios had booked Angel & Gabe in a Jazz Club in Storyville, the historic red light district of New Orleans, since it was the most popular nightclub area in the city. Most clubs were jazz clubs. This one was called the Crawfish, and the likes of Jelly Roll Morton and even Louis Armstrong had performed there. It was a popular cabaret and catered to a wide variety of locals and visitors.

Gabe was concerned that their style of Mexican cowboy music might be rejected. Juan reassured them that Gabe and Angel, backed by the Heavenly Host, would be welcome anywhere. The audience was primarily a deep south, Bible belt, God-loving group, even though they were almost all heavy drinkers.

When they perused the venue, Angel looked at Gabe and Juan and said softly, "It can't be any tougher than the Drag-On-Inn!" With a round of laughter, they all agreed.

Gabe added, "Plus, if there is trouble, we have good Karma," as he leaned down and scratched Karma's ears. They had cleaned Karma's wounds up as well as could be, and he was welcome at the Hotel. The owner said, "Sure; he is in better condition than most of our guests," referring to the rough and rowdy crowd that frequented the Storyville bordellos area.

The stage was not bad, and there was a big, black bouncer named Bubba. He told Juan Di Dios, "I just be here for back up," which seemed like a good idea.

It took about ten minutes to quiet the first audience with Gabe and the Host performing some jazzed up Hispanic instrumentals. The audience was restless. Some guy yelled, "What's with the dog on stage?"

Gabe responded with a smile. "He's good Karma. Come on up and pet him."

The smartass shut up and swigged down a warm Hurricane, a popular drink at the time.

When Gabe introduced Angel, the mood changed completely. The loud-mouthed one shouted again, "What the hell is the dog there for?

Gabe said, "You seem to be a pretty nice guy; what's your name?"

"Oddie!"

Gabe turned his head sideways and said, "Bubba, would you please throw Oddie out?"

Juan Di Dios whispered to Gabe, "Nice to have friends here, southern hospitality . . ."

Bubba firmly grabbed the obnoxious customer by the collar and the seat of the pants and physically threw him out. "See ya'll in church," he said, being a religious man.

When Angel began to sing *Summertime*, which had been a national favorite for a couple of years, the entire room was graciously and obediently at her command.

And then someone from a table full of Hawaiians yelled, "Angel, can you sing *Aloha Oi*?"

It was a song both Gabe and Angel had really enjoyed since the first time they heard it. They both had an affinity for the song and for the paradise from which it came. Gabe had introduced Angel to the song and told her it was composed by the last Queen of Hawaii, Liliuokalani, and Cheska had told him, "I will try and honor her." And she absolutely did.

Once again the audience was speechless, as spellbound as was Gabe. He kept thinking as he had since he had first seen her, that she was indeed a divine angel.

This time together was the first vacation they had had since Angie was born. And they missed her desperately. But at the conclusion of the last set, and after a long, standing ovation from an inebriated but totally enthralled audience, Gabe and Cheska walked swiftly the two blocks to the Ragin' Cajun Hotel. Gabe carried his guitar and conga drum, and Cheska had her huge costume bag over her shoulder.

They had the best room in the house. Gabe showered quickly and climbed into bed. When Cheska emerged from her shower, Gabe's mouth fell open. She was wearing peach, rayon, lingerie panties and no top, with a stunning flower lei around her neck, lying over her lovely breasts. "Aloha, señor."

"Aloha." She took his breath away; Gabe was speechless, but just for a moment.

"I have dreamed of you like this, your long, shiny black hair over your breasts, with a sweet-smelling flower lei. I saw this in my dream." And then he paused, looked down and up and thought to himself, "The girl of my dreams . . . "

"A lei." He paused again. *Lei, Laya . . . what does it mean?* he thought. He trailed off and gazed again at Angel.

"Where did you get the lei, darling?"

One of the men from the table of Hawaiians came to me after our second set and said it was an Aloha gift for singing Queen Lillokalani's song.

Gabe stood up slowly and stepped close to the love of his life. He put his hands on her waist and ran

109

them slowly up to her longing breasts. Diving deep into a long overdue passionate interlude, Angel moaned in ecstasy.

The night was a long, slow movement deeper and deeper into blissful, unbridled lovemaking. It represented lifetimes of passionate love and joyful exchanges of endless kisses and caresses. The humid, southern night air and endless passion covered them in perspiration. After some time, they sat naked on the bed with their legs crossed, facing each other, just gazing into the universe of each other's eyes. Every once in a while, Angel's eye would start twitching. Gabe said, "Are you nervous or excited?" She smiled her incomparable, dimpled grin and said, "I'm in heaven!"

When the first explosion occurred, it was in the kitchen of the hotel restaurant, where a gas main had been leaking. But the next explosion was from an unknown source in the alley. Gabe and Cheska thought they heard something but just held each other's hands in the dim light. When the sparks from the alley explosion burst the kitchen window, it was only seconds before the second explosion hit like a bomb. It blew a huge hole in the floor next to their bed, and the entire side of the building collapsed. An instant before the end, they both saw themselves as little, black-haired children in an earthquake next to a dry, rocky hill in broad daylight. They knew it was the passing of another lifetime together. They squeezed each other's hands and closed their eyes.

The very next moment, everything changed. In a fraction of a second, they were walking together in

110

an empyrean forest of gossamer trees vaguely like the woods they had strolled through in San Antonio a few years earlier, but otherworldly. They stopped and looked at each other, still holding hands, filled with passion of a different kind. It was completely ethereal. Smiling broadly, they seemed translucent, still the same, but in a gentle, turquoise light that permeated the landscape and sky in all directions. They felt each other's bodies, but not with their hands. The world was suddenly a different place, a truly transcendent place. Everything was perfect. They had never felt so good. As they began to look around, it was like a kaleidoscope of pastel colors slowly changing chromatically from moment to moment, with heavenly, warm breezes surrounding and caressing them, and they could taste sweetness with every breath. Every swallow was sweeter than honey nectar dripping down their throats. They felt ecstatically happy as they walked through tall, gentle grass that caressed their feet and legs and then their entire bodies.

Soon the grass was above their heads and turning an aqua blue, engulfing them like a warm ocean of pure ambrosial syrup. They were swept up on a tide of joy and bliss that surpassed anything they had ever felt or imagined in life.

They were still holding hands but feeling a parting. Their images of each other were dissolving, separating them physically, but not their spirits. They were smiling and looking into each other's eyes. They said, "I love you," simultaneously, knowing somehow that their love was in God's hands and that they would be together again. For a brief moment they saw baby Angelica in the arms of Mario. And they knew she would be all right.

They dissolved into a star field of a million universes, an endless cosmos, Gabe and Angel each going their own way for the next step in their unfoldment, when they would reunite. And they knew it as they blew kisses and faded to a blissful respite until the next incarnation.

The headline in the New Orleans Times Picayune the next morning reported that nine people had perished in the unexplained series of explosions. Ironically, the entertainment review was exclusively about the fantastic, new, Mexican-American "Jazz" group starring Gabe and Angel Mateo and their backup group, the Heavenly Host.

When the news got back to Austin, Mario was at Gabe's house as soon as he could get there. The sorrow and grief that surrounded the Mateos was beyond belief. All of them cried unceasingly, lovingly passing baby Angie around, but at their wits' ends. Mario seemed to be able to take charge better than anyone, and with his new bride, Britney, they offered to stay and care for Angie at Gabe's bungalow until things settled down. It was decided that this would be the best solution. But they all knew the shock would never entirely wear off.

A week after the explosion, more details surfaced and burial arrangements were finally made for the beloved Gabe and Angel. As it happened, the Heavenly Host had been staying in a different hotel with Juan Di Dios Fernando A. Saddened but grateful, they were all there alive. Services were held at the Texas State Cemetery. There were a hundred and forty friends and fans, from Austin and San Antonio. Tears were in every eye, as the couple was dearly loved and admired. The Heavenly Host played an instrumental rendition of *Amazing Grace*. The Mateos stood with Mario, Britney and baby Angela. After the closing prayer was uttered by Antoinette's priest from San Antonio, Father Perez Rodriguez asked for a moment of silence. While the heads were still bowed and tears still quietly flowing, Britney heard Mario tearfully whisper, "Karma." Eyes still closed, she nodded affirmatively. And then in a cracking voice, louder, she heard, "No, it's Karma!" It penetrated the reverent silence. And then one more time as Mario took his arm from around Britney, who was holding Angelica tightly, and ran up the side of the cemetery hill. "It's Karma!"

Ragged and dirty, with infected burns on his back and side and scabs on the front of his rear legs, he was twenty pounds lighter, a startling but awesome sight to see. Karma had found his way home. Mario fell on his knees beside the blessed dog and hugged him closely. Shortly thereafter, the crowd was gathering around the famous dog, already renowned in Austin for chewing on Sammy, who had offended everyone in town. When Britney gently held the little Angelica near Karma, the dog's eyes filled with tears as he delicately sniffed her, his eyes looking up and around for approval, although his heart told him to lick her tiny face to let her know he came back for Gabe and Angel to watch over her.

He didn't; she knew already. After surviving a hellacious journey, the legendary dog was finally home . . . Karma was good.

Chapter Eight

Karma

After the funeral, Ramiero and Antoinette kept Angie and Karma for a short while. Karma regained his health but would only run beside Ramiero's horse when it was hooked to the wagon, and Antoinette was holding Angie in the wagon. Although most everyone in the county had cars by then, it was still cowboy country, and a buckboard was not uncommon on the dirt roads. So evening rides happened more for Karma's sake than the Mateos', and because everyone knew the legend of Gabe and Angel, folks would wave and holler, "Howdy, Angie," or "Hola, Karma."

The grandparents knew they could not keep Angie. Mario and Britney could not have children and already adored the baby as if she were their own. Six months after the unforgettable service and sadness of the horrendous series of events, Mario got a fabulous job offer. World War II was imminent; jobs were scarce, and the offer was from a marketing department of the Builders Exchange on Main Street in a little-known country town called Santa Ana in southern California.

It was decided that Mario and Britney would adopt the baby and take the job. Karma would go with them, of course. In spite of his increasing age, Karma was as unconditionally loving as ever and still a bit frisky. As a well-known fence jumper, he was able to start associating with a giant champagne-colored poodle, who was even bigger in height than he was. Her name, Fifi, would have been more appropriate for a toy poodle, but love is blind, and before anyone realized such a thing could happen, Fifi was pregnant.

Fifi's owners were big fans of Karma and proudly offered the puppies for sale as Karma's litter. In honor of Gabe and Angel, they first offered the Mateos their pick of the litter. Antoinette immediately turned the honor over to Britney and Mario. There was no doubt the biggest puppy was so much like Karma, it was understood that he was the chosen one, and that his name should be Karma as well.

Mario told Ramiero that he probably could not take the puppy and Karma to his new home in rural Santa Ana. Ramiero quite frankly said, "Bueno, dile al perro" (tell the dog). Deep down Mario knew that to take Angie away from Karma would kill him, so, of course, Mario ended up taking both Karma and the puppy.

When the time came to make the move, Mario had a new Chevy Suburban truck. The puppy was four months old and already weighed forty pounds; Karma had some trouble being patient with him. When Mario and Britney got the truck loaded, they made a space in the back for Karma and Karma 2. Karma didn't like it, but he was old and tired. But before he would let Mario put him in the back of the truck, he had to see Britney get in the front with Angie, who was now a tiny toddler. This had become a policy whenever they would all go somewhere in the new truck.

When they were finally ready for the trek across west Texas to Lubbock and then due west to California, a group gathered at the Mateo's house to say goodbye to the young family, who had become such an indelible part of the legend of Gabe, Angel, and Karma. Friends, neighbors, and fans were all there to wave goodbye and send the young family off with love and prayers. Even Fifi was there. After all, she was destined to become part of the legend.

Every hundred miles or so Mario would stop the truck and let the dogs out. The puppy would romp and play and stand in one spot and pee without lifting his leg. Karma would watch him and think, *Puppy brain; he has a lot to learn yet.*

Old Karma moved much slower than ever before, and Mario knew the heat was hard on him, so he had the back door propped open a few inches and secured with blocks and ropes so it would not open all the way.

Even so, each time they stopped, Karma was looking a little weaker. The puppy was full of pep and anxious to get out and run, but Mario had to start helping Karma get down over the bumper and back into the Suburban. The longer they drove, the more concerned Mario became with Karma. The panhandle plains south of Lubbock seem to go on forever. Even finding a small town for gas or a motel was a challenge.

It was dusk and still many miles to go before the next town. Fortunately, Britney had packed as much food and drink as she could at the previous stop. Mario decided to make one more stop, mostly for Karma. It was 90 degrees, and everyone was hot and exhausted. Naturally, both Mario and Britney were anxious to get to Lubbock, where they had reservations for the new Hotel Lubbock. Angie seemed to be doing fine, but she was still just a toddler, and they wanted to make the trip as easy as possible for her, of course.

Mario found a natural rest stop off the old two-lane highway going north towards Lubbock, and pulled 100 feet off the road. It was sweltering and dusty. After Mario helped Karma out of the truck, he assisted Britney and Angie. Ramiero had built a little upright cradle chair for Angie, so she could sit off the ground. It was quite ingenious for the times. Mario kicked some tumbleweed out of the way, and used his shovel to clear a space where they could spread out two blankets and set down the picnic basket. Britney immediately sat down on a pillow next to Angie and started to feed her some little treats like apple pieces and goat cheese from *Ganny*, which is what she called her grandmother.

Karma was lying on his side, breathing heavily as Mario lifted the dog's weary head up and held a handful of water to his muzzle. Mario's eyes were tearing up.

"Britney, we can't let Karma die out here in the plains. He is royalty; a hero."

"Mario, it might be his time. He is a pretty old dog, and he doesn't look good right now."

"I know, I know. I worry about even getting him back in the rig for the road."

The puppy had been running around in the bushes but returned, lapped up some water, and lay down with his head between his front paws looking at Karma, blinking his eyes. Karma was king of the world to little Karma.

Mario crawled a few feet over onto the blanket next to Britney. Drinking a lukewarm coke and eating a few bites of cheese helped refresh the big man.

"You know, Britney, I never told the people at the Hotel Lubbock that we have a dog, uh, dogs. I kind of thought we would leave them in the suburban at night."

"Yeah, I guess I did, too." She looked over at Karma. The great animal was surely dying.

"I can't stand this, Britney." He pushed himself up onto his knees and stood up. Then he straddled Karma and lifted his body above the water bowl as well has he could. Karma tried to steady his legs.

The puppy stood up and scooted over next to Angie. Angie giggled; she loved the puppy. Karma emitted an unexpected growl as he looked up at the baby and the puppy.

"Britney," said Mario, "I think papa Karma is jealous." He smiled, trying to ease the tension.

Almost instantly the growl turned into a vicious snarl as Karma launched himself directly at the puppy and the baby. It happened so fast that Britney grabbed Angie by the front of her pinafore and yanked her away as Karma's huge jaws shot just to the right of the child, knocking little Karma aside and biting viciously into the back of a seven foot Diamondback rattlesnake.

Once his teeth were instantly buried into the reptile's body, Karma quickly picked it up and kept charging straight away from the area. The snake rattled and struck Karma in the side with a dose of venom that would have killed a horse. The two animals spasmodically rolled over three times before landing with the snake wrapped around Karma and Karma's jaws locked on the dead snake.

By this time Mario had grabbed Britney and the baby and stumbled back to the truck. The scene of the dog and snake was a convoluted, gory mess.

Mario helped Britney and Angie back into the front seat of the truck and began the grizzly work of cutting the snake off Karma's body.

He carried the snake body parts fifty feet away and threw them as far as he could, then spent the next hour in the west Texas moonlight, digging a grave for the most magnificent dog he had ever known.

His eyes filled with tears as he pulled Karma's body onto the picnic blanket and then into the grave. Britney stood back while he threw the dirt over the blanket-covered body and filled the grave to ground level.

He turned to Britney and said, "Karma wouldn't have died here if he had known how hard it would be for me to dig this grave!"

She smiled a little. Mario was exhausted and decided that they would settle in for the night in the back of the truck and leave in the morning.

Coyotes howled in happiness as they chewed up the gnarly remains of the monstrous Diamondback.

As is typical in west Texas, the sunrise was spectacular, and after getting everything ready to proceed onto Lubbock, Mario suggested they have a little service for Karma. Britney agreed.

The sun was rising against a steel grey-blue sky and lighting up the desert like a great torch.
.

With bowed head Mario reverently spoke softly, "Heavenly father, this here animal was the most incredible hero I have ever known. He protected us from the lowlife Sammy and has now saved Angel and Gabe's baby from a deadly serpent. I know he died happy, and God, please let Gabe and Angel meet him in heaven; he deserves it. God bless Karma; Amen."

The drive to Lubbock and eventually to California was long and hot, but Mario, Britney, Angelica, and little Karma were safe and sound upon arrival in Santa Ana.

Chapter Nine

Carl Atman

California USA

It was a typically dry, windy day when Carl was born. His father, Bud Atman, managed orange groves in Orange County. California. He worked for an orchard and grove management company, Ron Rayl's Services, LLC, where his primary job was to take care of the 80-some smudge pots that were strategically placed among the trees to warm the areas on chilly nights. Orange County was mostly farm land in those days. Little did Bud realize that someday the creator of Mickey Mouse, Walt Disney, would build his famous Disneyland on the very site where the Orange groves seem to go on in all directions when Betty Jean gave birth to her sweet son, Carl.

Carl was a quiet baby, but in an introspective way, like he was contemplating, not just drooling; a plump, happy child, never angry or fussy or cranky about anything. He was the only child that Betty Jean and Bud Atman would ever have, and he was a lucky boy to have them as his parents. He was the light of their eyes. Carl was intelligent and perceptive. Although by all standards, he was indulged, but not with the usual negative results caused by spoiling a child. He was such a sweet and good natured boy that anyone who met him wanted to make him happy and see his infectious smile as a reward. As the boy grew, Bud and Betty Jean were amazed at how generous Carl was with everything he had, whether it was sharing a toy or just little things that kids never do for adults, like opening doors. His manners were just like his parents', polite and sincere. By five years of age, Carl had met some friends in the neighborhood and had a congenial little social life. Here again, his folks could not have been more pleased with the way he shared his favorite things, and seemed to want to make everybody else happy.

Bud and Jean had begun studying various religions when they first met. They were in their twenties and both searching for the right path to follow. So Carl was being brought up in a family that was not strict about religion at all. They told him that there was a God, and he was free to go to any church he so desired. Betty Jean had been a Presbyterian, attending church occasionally at the whim of her parents, who usually figured that they *should* go because it was good to do "something religious" every Sunday. Ultimately, Bud and Betty Jean were open to finding a spiritual path that Carl would choose to follow.

So Sunday was a day of excitement for the family because they would attend different churches. Carl seemed very interested in each church, paying attention all the way through and trying to sing along with the hymns, looking up at mom and dad with a big smile.

At six-years-old, Carl began telling his parents about his amazing dreams. He told stories of wolves in the frozen tundra and soldiers in the revolutionary war and the civil war. He would talk about beaches with black sand. Bud and Betty Jean were amazed. These were pre-TV days. And although there were magazines around the house, neither one could ever equate one of Carl's stories with any radio show, newspaper or magazine they had seen. So naturally they were mystified.

Most of Carl's stories were short but like vivid memories, some with happy endings, some not, and some just relaying facts about things he had seen in his dreams. Occasionally, there was a violent story like the one about a horrible storm and boat full of dying, bloody pigs. This shocked Bud and Betty Jean, as they had never mentioned anything bloody to Carl. Of course Carl had heard things in church about Christ being crucified and "the blood and the body," but they didn't think that had any relevance to Carl's stories.

Overall, the stories were surprisingly unique but consistent, like memories, not passing dreams; it was very intriguing.

They knew they had a smart, creative kid. And every day was an adventure with little Carl Atman.

One day in the spring, there was a company picnic held at Orange City Park. The company that Bud worked for was merging with another company, but it was a big secret as to what company was being approached for this opportunity, although there were rumors in the grapevine.

The event was attended by more than seventy people, at which Mr. Ron Rayl, a lean, handsome young man with a shock of dark blonde hair, stood up on a small bandstand and introduced the president of Farms United. The crowd cheered in unison and applauded loudly. They had heard of the potential merger partner and knew that this meant imminent growth for both companies in the burgeoning farm and orchard industry of Orange County.

Families were happily meeting and mixing. Kids were playing hopscotch, jump rope and tetherball. The older children were on the volleyball and basketball courts. Some of the bigger boys were playing football. Eight-year-old Carl was excited about meeting other children and ventured into the crowds of youngsters.

A teenage boy chasing a football ran into him, and both of them hit the ground. With no remorse the teenager stood up, grabbed the ball, and as Carl stood up trembling, the big boy, flaunting his macho side, squatted down in front of him and said, "Look kid; this game is for the big guys and not a little snot-faced kid like you." Then he poked his finger in Carl's chest hard, pushing him back down. Carl didn't make a noise; tears just ran from his hazel eyes. The big boy laughed and looked back at his group of chums.

But as he stepped backward, he suddenly found himself falling over something. There was a very large, motley-looking dog standing in between them right beside Carl. Carl hadn't noticed the dog until the rude boy fell back on his fanny and lay there looking up at the huge dog with the wide jaw, emitting a low, threatening growl.

Carl looked up at the dog and back at the trouble-maker and started to laugh. He pushed himself up and wrapped his arm around the dog's neck, totally unafraid, as if it were his pet.

By then a small crowd had gathered, and Bud stood in amazement at Carl. Carl had never had a dog. In fact, they had definitely decided not to get one until he was older. But they could see that he identified with the enormous, old dog, which stood faithfully beside him.

"He's my dog," said a tall, black-haired girl, perhaps two years older than Carl, standing behind the dog.
"His name is Karma."

Then she petted her dog and with a knowing grin said, "Good Karma!"

Carl looked at his father and said, "Karma . . . dad, it means, do the right thing and good things will happen to you, and do the wrong things and bad things will happen." Then he paused and looked at the bully standing in the background. "Like what happened to him." He pointed at the obnoxious bully.

The crowd loved the gutsy boy and his stalwart companion, Karma.

Bud and Betty Jean had no idea where he had learned such a thing. In a few minutes Mario and Britney were shaking hands with Bud and Betty Jean. Before too long Bud and Betty heard the legend of Karma, senior, right up to his sacrificing his life by saving Angie from the deadly rattler in the plains of the Texas panhandle. They were enthralled.

Betty Jean felt like she had been at fault by taking her eyes off Carl earlier. Then suddenly she said, "Where are the children?"

Britney responded gently, "Don't worry, they are with Karma." And she pointed to them walking together.

Carl and Angie were getting acquainted with each other. She was older and taller than Carl, but they were instant friends, like long lost family, although unaware of their soul kinship. They walked around their folks and towards the tennis courts, right through the football players, with Karma in between them.

The teenage boys graciously stepped back as Karma slowly swung his head from side to side like a mountain lion strolling across the Serengeti, looking for prey. He knew he was on double duty.

It turned out that Bud and Betty found a house near theirs for rent and contacted Mario and Britney. Soon they were neighbors. So it was not unusual that Carl and Angie spent a lot of time together, always with Karma. They became the best of friends. Even though Angie was older than Carl, she looked up to him. She knew he was extremely smart and lovingly called him, "Big brother."

It was inevitable but eventually the time came, a sad day indeed, when Karma didn't wake up. No one knew what happened to him. The vet said, "He was a very old dog and had a full life."

They all knew it was true, but there was no holding back the grief. Mario had a large yard with several California lemon trees, and a six-foot, grey, slump stone fence surrounding the back yard, and the three-bedroom house. The front yard had a white picket fence with a simple gate on the side and four rows of rosebushes Britney had planted and lovingly tended.

Mario insisted that he bury Karma in his yard. Some neighbors didn't like the idea. One of them asked him,
"Why would you bury your old dog in the yard?"

Carl was standing beside Mario with Angie. "Because it's good karma!"

Mario told the nosy neighbor, "If you could live a life one-tenth as pure as Karma did, you would be a saint." Then he stepped closer to the slender neighbor, bumping him unintentionally with his generous belly, and said, "You are invited to the service."

Many neighbors and friends gathered after Mario had dug a grave big enough to accommodate the plywood coffin he had built for his loving dog. Bud and Mario and two other men lifted the box up by straps underneath it and lowered it into the grave. Mario told the brief story of Karma, senior, and Karma, the second, adding sadly, "I guess this will be the last Karma," before proceeding to fill in the grave with dirt. He had a simple wooden cross he proudly secured in the dirt. When Mario made the cross, he wanted to commemorate both Karmas, and since he still had the original leather collar from Karma's father, he screwed it to the crosspiece and varnished it, and it seemed almost as clear as the first day Gabriel Mateo had seen the named burned into the leather: KARMA.

Mario finished his little speech about Karma with tears in his eyes, then said, "One of our daughter's best friends, Carl Atman, asked if he could say something, and then Angie would like to sing a little song."

The small crowd was as solemn as they would have been at a service for a family member.

Carl proudly stood up by the grave and said, "I've been reading a lot about karma lately, not our friend, Karma, but karma, the philosophy. And even though this Karma was just a dog, he lived as though he knew what good karma and bad karma were all about, basically that what goes around comes around! Something we should all think about all the time." He said his piece and went back to his folding chair.

Everyone was shocked that such a young boy could be so well spoken. Then Angie, who had been learning a special song in the church choir, stood up and began to sing an ancient hymn that many people knew.

"Amazing grace, how sweet thou art . . . "

Britney whispered to Mario, "I didn't know she knew that song." Mario whispered back to her that she had probably learned it from Britney. She sang it almost as sweetly as her mother, Angel.

As the years rolled on, Carl and Angie remained best friends. Their bond was as much like loving brother and sister as the real thing could possibly be.

Angie had the gracious beauty of her Italian mother and the strong Hispanic influence of her handsome father, Gabriel. She became a stunning teenager, the head of the pep squad. In California in those days, there were really only two ethnic groups in school, the white kids and the "Mexican" kids. This was before the politically-correct term *Hispanic* came into use.

Because Mario was also of Italian heritage like his sister, Francesca, most people never thought much about whether Angelica was Mexican or not, they just assumed she was. She began dating a boy named Abraham Finkelstein, the class genius. Abraham means *exalted father* in Hebrew. He was the only Jewish boy in the school. The kids called him "Brainiac," but not to his face. He was shy and sweet-natured. He might have been harassed by other boys in the school except he was six-foot, five-inches tall. His black, curly hair and wide shoulders made him look even bigger.

The basketball coach practically begged him to play on the team. He was more than an inch taller than Jerry West of the then famous Los Angeles Lakers.

But Abraham had his sights on going to UCLA as an academic and, in the back of his mind, eventually marrying Angie.

Angie confided in Carl that she loved Abe. Carl was a freshman and Abe a senior, but they had become friends as they were both in the Latin club and the math club. Carl thought Abe was perfect for Angie and told her that he approved. Angie was also a senior. Abe had, not surprisingly, been compared to Abe Lincoln, not only because of his intellect and size but because on a dare, he had proved he could hold a twenty-pound axe straight out at arm's length for several minutes, an impressive stunt for which the 16th President had become legendary.

Two years after graduation, Abe had secured a good part-time job in LA and asked Angie to marry him. Everyone approved. Carl was asked to be the best man at the wedding. He was definitely lonely when Angie moved away. By then he was a senior and trying to decide what to do with his life. Always introspective since childhood, he kept to himself quite a bit. He had studied the various religions and tried his best to understand the vast differences and at the same time the similarities between the major religions of the world.

Carl had repeated dreams about being a small child, meditating in some ancient forest with another dark-skinned child, sitting crossed-legged and chanting, "Jai Krishna" repeatedly. He tried it several times. Once while sitting in the foothills in the late afternoon, he tried it again. He had heard that mystics would meditate on the third eye, the space between the eyebrows, and that this third eye would appear as a glowing, golden orb or star with a dark blue background, if one had meditated long enough.

At one point after spending five or ten minutes trying to focus on this phenomenon and also a few minutes listening to the sound of *Om*, a kind of cosmic humming noise, he heard little and saw nothing but was getting cold. When he opened his eyes, it was dark. He looked at his watch and realized that what he thought had been a few minutes was about an hour and a half.

He was near his car and there was ambient light, so he walked slowly to the vehicle. But he was astounded that so much time had passed. As he strolled slowly to his car, he felt light of foot and a great peace within. It was something he had never experienced before. He drove directly to the library and perused several books about meditation. One such book was based on quotes by a man called Swami Paramahansa Yogananda. The quote that struck him as being so appropriate for him and intense at that moment was: "Peace is God's breath of immortality in you."

He left the library with a whole new concept of inner peace. It was an epiphany, a life-changing moment in his search for something greater than Carl Atman. And on the same shelf, he ran across a book called, *How to Know God (The Yoga Aphorisms of Patanjali)* with comments by Swami Pradhadamanda and Swami Vivekananda, another Indian who had come to the US in 1893, the same year Yogananda was born in India.

He discovered that Sanskrit was the oldest language in the world and the basis for 97 percent of the languages used worldwide. He was stunned to find out in Vivekanda's book that Atman, his own name, was an ancient Sanskrit term that meant soul. If he wasn't already convinced, curious, and excited, he now felt he knew there was a lot more to life than what he had learned or suspected thus far.

The awesome day had changed his life. He was humbled by the use of the term Atman and determined to learn more. He left the library a wiser young man, knowing that he needed to find the right spiritual teacher, what the Hindus call a Guru.

Carl was a natural musician and had developed a wonderful style of finger picking on his Goya guitar. Mario had told him many times about how great Angie's father, Gabe, was on guitar and how Gabe and Francesca wowed the audiences on stage. When Mario would tell Carl about the undying love they had for each other, Carl was enchanted. "Was your sister that beautiful, Mario?"

"Well, Carl, you see how beautiful Angie is? Her mother was equally lovely."

More than once Carl asked Mario, "Do you think I will ever find a girl that lovely who will love me as much?"

Carl was now eighteen. He was at the top of his class.
He was athletic but didn't play on any of the teams. He was a good-looking young man by any standards and well liked. Mario always liked Carl and had

become very close to him, as Carl and Angie had grown to be such good friends over the years.

"What are you looking for in life, Carl?"

"Honestly, Mario, it's pretty simple. I know now I want to understand more about God. I want to make the right career choice. As I told you, I think I will study conservation in college. I think there is an imminent environmental disaster brewing for this blue and green planet of ours, and I would like to help curb that. I want to find the woman of my dreams, who wants to spend the rest of this life and every life I live after that with me."

Mario looked curiously at Carl. "You believe in reincarnation?"

"I have read a lot about it, Mario, and the concept has been a belief for thousands of years. From all I can see, nothing really dies, it just changes form. It happens around us all the time. Trees grow and die and wither away, and more trees grow. It happens with everything. Long story short, I believe it happens with every living thing. Yes, I do believe in reincarnation."

Mario looked at Carl seriously and said, "You remind me so much of Angie's father, Gabriel."

"You have told me that before. Thank you; I am flattered."

"Well, you look totally different, but you are handsome in your own right and talented like Gabe. But God knows, when I am with you, it feels like

135

being with Gabe so strongly sometimes, it's almost uncanny, like deja vu."

"Far out, Uncle Mario; I feel the same way about you. So, anyhow, the last big dream I have for the future of my life is this: I want to meet my soulmate. Of course, I want her to be beautiful, with a heart of gold, as lovely on the inside as the outside. It would be nice if she liked playing music and singing as well. I want to find the girl of my dreams and make a life with her, so there you have it, wha'da ya think?"

"I think you have a pretty good idea about the woman you want to meet. Have you had dreams about her?"

"Oh, my God, Mario, funny you should ask. I could write a book about the dreams I have had about this woman."

"Reincarnation, Carl?"

"Yes, Mario."

Mario looked down and said questioningly, "You could call it, *The Lives of Carl Atman?"*

"I could Mario, it's all here . . . in the Atman." He touched his forehead between his eyebrows with his forefinger and issued a little grin.

Mario grinned. "Tell me about her."

"Well, first of all, she is different and the same in all my dreams. In other words, she pretty much

136

looks the same: lovely . . . clef chin, sometimes blue eyes, sometimes brown. Big dimples. Her hair is mostly dark, but sometimes blonde. Her laugh is absolutely infectious and her smile would light up a cloudy day."

"Pretty nice, young man; anything more?"

"Well, Mario, I have never talked with anyone about this, really . . . well, maybe Angie a little. She is my best friend."

"Go ahead, Carl."

"It's all been just a tease. I see her in different clothes, in different places, speaking different languages. It always goes by so fast with each dream. And she looks different, but the same. Am I obsessed, Mario?"

"I don't know, Carl; sounds like you are busy manifesting your dream woman. Is there any one image of her that is more enduring than the others?"

"Yes. I have had this dream a few times. She is on a black sand beach in the tropics somewhere, maybe Hawaii. She is wearing some kind of grass skirt and no top, and she looks like a goddess, and oh, yeah, she had like a flower necklace. . . what do they call it, a *lei* around her neck. And this is weird, but sometimes her left eye is tweaked."

Mario said, "What?"

Carl said, "Hard to explain, but perfect none the less."

Mario put his hand to his chin as if concentrating a little more. "Carl, do you think that if you met this woman, you would know her?"

"Without a doubt, but it's just a dream . . ."

"You know, Carl, I was always overweight and had a poor self image. I never had a real girlfriend. I just dreamed that maybe someone could love me. When I met Britney, there was no question. I thought she was too beautiful and too good for me. Thank God she didn't think so. She treated me like gold, so whatever dream I ever had of any kind of woman before that was obliterated by the love that seemed to flow between us like honey from the moment we met. She became my dream and my reality of happiness. It's called love. So from personal experience in the soul mate department, dreams do come true, but as you know, never exactly as you imagine. When it happens, what you once imagined gratefully becomes cloudy and vague because what you manifested will be the real thing. Am I getting too esoteric, Carl?"

Carl shook his head. "Not for me, Uncle Mario. Makes perfect sense; thank you."

"I'm curious, Carl. Angie says you meditate sometimes with her. How does that work for you?"

"It makes me feel very calm and relaxed."

"And do you pray?"

"Yep, every day."

"Hmmmmmm, and you are good to people, right?'

"I try."

"Then, Carl, I believe you are crafting your life just perfectly. And all your dreams will come true. But the one thing I can remind you of is that, as I said, although dreams come true, they are never quite like you expect."

Carl smiled a gleaming grin that warmed Mario's heart; he wrapped his arms around Carl and gave him a loving bear hug. It felt just like hugging Gabe. Carl didn't see the tear. They stood for minute at arm's length like a father and son. There was a blink of Carl's eyes, and he saw Mario as Gabe would have seen him twenty-five years earlier. It was a flashback, but Carl didn't know it. He would never know he had been Gabe in a former life; it just doesn't come to pass that way. But they both knew something was going on.

"You know, Mario, I have done quite a bit of research, and you are going to laugh at this, but when you talk about reincarnation and such, my name has a particular meaning. In the Hindu world it means *life- giving soul* or *the real eternal self! God*!"

Mario looked totally amazed. He put his hand up to his chin again, holding it and thinking deeply as he often did and then spoke softly and ever so slow, "Are you telling me that Carl means God?"

"No, Mario, 'Atman.'"

"You know, I always said you were a nice looking guy, but you better watch that ego."

"In order to find the atman, one has to totally lose the ego; I'm not there yet. Okay, Mario, enough on religion," said Carl, with another grin, "except one more thing. I know you are Christian, but did you know there is a lot in the Bible about meditating. And there is a Christian term, the 'mystic union,' which corresponds with the Yoga concept that any person can unite with the Godhead or Atman through a perfect state of Yoga."

"Cool," said Mario. "It is an interesting point, Carl. I know you will find the perfect spiritual path for you because you have the desire, you are smart, and you are persistent. I think I will stick with Jesus for two reasons. First of all, I think He is the savior, and secondly Britney would leave me if I didn't believe Jesus saved my soul. Just between you and me, Carl, I believe God is a woman!"

"In India, they call God *Divine Mother*. And . . ." added Carl with a serious expression, "Namaste— the God in me bows to the God in you."

Mario laughed and countered with, "You know where it's at, man!"

Carl said, "Very cute."

Then like a minister in a revival, Mario said loudly, "Thank you, Jesus!"

After high school Carl attended Saddleback Junior College, where he studied world religions, classical guitar, and took an interesting new class called Thai Chi Chuan, a slow-moving, meditative exercise for relaxation, health, and self defense. He was drawn to the ancient Chinese traditional exercise in an unusual way. He loved the meditative aspect but didn't realize that he would be learning self-defense techniques as well. It was his favorite class.

He had a small apartment in El Toro, not far away from Irvine, California. Even though Carl had lived in the area for two years, he had not been to L.A. to visit Angie and Abraham, although they stayed in touch by phone and mail. Carl worked in the first health food store in the area, called *Mother Nature's Health Food*. His diet was good, and people liked him and trusted his advice. Occasionally he would sit in at a local coffee house called the *Mon Ami* and play guitar on Sunday afternoons during the jam session.

His idol was an up-and-coming young, blind guitar player/singer named Jose Feliciano, who played a Spanish instrumental called *Malagueña*, which Carl loved as if he had heard it a thousand times in another lifetime. Jose would always come on stage with his German shepherd, and Carl thought of Karma whenever he saw Jose perform, remembering Mario's stories about Gabe and Karma.

Overall, Carl was happy; he tried to meditate but nothing outstanding ever happened, like the day he meditated for an hour and a half. He felt lonely; even though he dated some affable young women and had a few friends at school, there was an enormous gap in his life. He attended some church services, but was never drawn into one particular kind of church, although he attended Christian churches, Jewish synagogues, Islamic mosques and others. He believed in Jesus as the Son of God, but also in reincarnation, which was generally not accepted among the Christians he met. He kept thinking about his epiphany in the foothills and that he should find a teacher and learn to meditate. His research told him that resurrection and reincarnation were synonymous. He was confused. When he heard there would be a new class called Yoga 1-A, he signed up immediately as he thought the class would be focused on meditation.

As it turned out, before the class started, someone told him it was about exercise like his Tai Chi class, so he decided he would cancel. When he went to bed that night, before he woke up, he had the longest dream of his life. He was trapped under an old- fashioned buckboard wagon; he was in extreme pain and burning up. He felt someone pulling on his leg. And then there was an infinite void of blackness and a star-filled sky, and he thought, "How can I see the sky if there is a wagon on top of me?" He stopped thinking as the most brilliant star in the sky was coming at him; it was glorious. And then suddenly he was sitting in a grass shack surrounded by a group of people he assumed were southern slaves. They were smiling and clapping their hands along with his own bare, calloused, black hands, beating a strange drum in his lap. The drum was made of a skin-covered shell. He marveled at it. Just before the dream ended, he was being caressed by his dream woman, as she softly sang a hymn, as his head lay against her warm breasts and her love enveloped him.

Carl awoke with a start, immediately flipped over and tried to go back to sleep. But the dream was over. The celestial woman was gone, and he was alone.

For some reason, he knew not why, he decided to take the Hatha Yoga class, which was to be taught by a man named Yogi Thon, which sounded to Carl like Yogathon, a long, tiring event.

Two hours before the evening class after Carl had taken a long walk in the foothills nearby, he returned, took a shower, and got an unexpected call from Angie. He was delighted to hear that Abe and Angie would be coming down in a couple of hours. He told them that he had a Yoga class at Saddleback at 7pm, but he should be finished by 8pm and would meet them at the Red Onion in El Toro. There was lot of catching up to do.

After going back and forth about canceling, Carl finally figured he would take the class, and if it turned into a Yogathon, he would slide out the back door.

He arrived at twilight, and coincidently heard the classic rock song *Twilight Time* by the Platters on his radio, which was made popular a few years before:

> *Heavenly shades of night are falling, it's twilight time;*
> *Out of the mist your voice is calling, it's twilight time.*
> *When purple-colored curtains mark the end of day,*

I'll hear you, my dear, at twilight time.

He had always loved the song and imagined someday he might share his feelings about it with his dream girl. Deep down, he had hoped there would be a lovely young woman in the class like the one on the black sand beach in his dreams. "Fat chance," he thought. "Oh, well, I will be able to focus on the class more if it's only old Yogi Thon."

The signs were pretty clear: *YOGA* with arrows ending up at an open door near the end of the hallway. There didn't seem to be anyone else around as he walked in. It was just him and a woman facing a blackboard. His first impression of the incredibly well-built individual in the tight yoga pants was, "If this is Yogi Thon, I might have to take this class, after all."

"Excuse me, miss, I am here for the Hatha Yoga class." She was writing something on the blackboard.

"Just a minute, please."

As he drew closer, his nostrils were filled with the aroma of fresh Hawaiian plumeria flowers, like those used in lei in the islands. Her long, black hair was tied back in a ponytail and lay neatly on a light green cashmere sweater.

After the first sight of her and the way her essence of flowers filled his senses, he felt a bit shaky. He walked up behind her, standing about a foot away.

144

She spoke softly, not turning around as she finished writing *YOGA CLASS CANCELLED*. Then she seemed to turn ever so slowly on purpose. She was not really trying to tantalize him, but it was too late not to when he looked at her, face to face.

Time stood still. Never before had either one of them, in this life or any other, just stood in awe of someone they had just met, for a few long and unforgettable minutes.

She wore no makeup. Her lips were full and naturally red. Her tanned face with dimpled cheeks blushed. Carl had to stand back in awe.

The young woman was mesmerized. Before her stood a breathtaking young man. Not only struck by his physical characteristics, she imagined that she saw a glow around him, an aura. Her feelings ran deep inside, and she felt an uncanny warmth embrace her, which accounted for the mantling of her shapely cheeks. She had seen him in her dreams.

"Do we know each other?" mumbled Carl, while his eyes looked into the endless beauty of the dream that was alive and inches away from him.

"I don't know," she said in a soft, unintentionally sultry voice. It warmed Carl inside and out, he felt a little dizzy.

And then, as they stood feeling enthralled and overcome as if they had known each other for a thousand years, Carl noticed that she had two different colored eyes. The left eye was brown, and the right eye was an incredible aqua blue.

"My eyes are weird," she said, looking down. He put his hand under her chin, lifting it up, and said, "Your eyes are perfect."

"Weird," she repeated. "My father was a Cyclops!"

Carl said, "Jesus said, 'When thine eye be single, thy whole body shall be full of light.'"

"Funny you should say that; in reality my father is a Yogi."

"Yogi Thon?" he questioned.

She added softly with a little smile, "Not really, it's like his stage name, but he is a spiritually evolved man, a saint for sure, and he has taught me much about the third eye."

"I've been meditating since I was a child."

"Perfect!"

She pointed to her left eye and then her right. "What color do you prefer, brown or blue? Go ahead, pick one."

"I can't."

"Please do," she said.

"Okay. . . blue."

At that moment she winked the brown eye and kept it shut for a moment, just looking straight ahead at him with the glowing blue iris.

Carl knew his heart skipped a beat and then another. He was practically hypnotized. "So," he said, trying to regain his composure, "Where is Yogi Thon?"

"He had other business that came up and knew there was a lack of sign-ups and asked if I could take his place. And now there's no one but you."

"Jai Guru," or, I mean, "Thank God," Carl thought.

"What is it with us?" she struggled for words. "What is your name?"

"Atman."

This time she seemed pleasingly taken aback. "Like the eternal soul kind of Atman?"

"No," said Carl, with a smile that totally enchanted her again. "Like in Carl."

"Nice to meet you, Carl."

She held out her right hand. They touched. It was what they both expected, magic, chills, and warm rushes of excitement, sexually and spiritually.

"And your name?"

"Serenity."

"Peace and love."

"Something like that. Tell me, Mr. Atman, why do I feel like I have known you forever?"

"That is a good question, Serenity; I think we should discuss this more, perhaps somewhere else . . . I love your name."

"That's fine with me." Serenity smiled an ear to ear smile that illuminated a glow around her like a halo, and Carl's knees felt weak again. What he didn't know was that Serenity, although appearing to be very calm and cool, could hardly control the rapid pace of her heart.

"Ever been to the Red Onion in El Toro?"

"Sounds like a Chinese place."

"Uh, no, it's Mexican food. . . "

"Duh; let me lock up, and we'll go. May I follow you in my V-dub?"

"You betcha. I saw a white bug parked near my car; Serenity, I'm in the red '64 Pontiac GTO convertible.

"I'm impressed; maybe we should just go in your car if I can bring my puppy?"

"You can bring anything you like."

"I like my puppy; I just got him from the Humane Society. He's only four months old; he looked so lonely, and I was lonely." Feeling as if she had slipped, she looked over at Carl.

He didn't hesitate. "Not any more," he said. And then, as if he had been too bold, he added. "I mean, now you, uh, have the new puppy."

"I know what you meant, Mr. Atman."

"Well, what's the puppy's name?"

"No name, really; they called him 'Big Fella' at the pound, but that sounds too much like a horse. Will you mind him in your GTO?"

"No worries, Serenity. We can put the top up when we are at the Red Onion. I guess I got the car because I had wild dreams for years that I was driving a red '32 Ford roadster, and it turned into this GTO. Silly dream, but when I saw it, I had to have it." What he didn't add was that the girl in the car was strangely like Serenity. It was all simply too uncanny.

As they locked up the classroom door and strolled down the hallway, Serenity took Carl's hand. He looked at their hands and at her precious face as she continued to talk. "I . . . I have some kind of fear of hallways. Plus when I arrived, there were a couple of gnarly biker dudes making smart remarks at me."

"No problem, young lady, you are with the right man. I can be pretty tough on gnarly dudes when they try to upset my Serenity." He grinned, and so did she.

They walked quietly around a corner, and the two "dudes" were waiting, apparently for her. They were indeed bikers, in full regalia, worn-out jeans, and black leather jackets. They were both six-footers; one was pretty stocky. He turned and displayed his Hell's Angel logo on the back of his jacket, whirled around and looked directly at Carl.

"You look like a frat boy; don't you have business with the other frat assholes?"

Carl stopped, as had Serenity, and he gently put his arm in front of her and moved her behind him.

He didn't know whether his training in Tai Chi would help him defend himself and his newly found love, but he felt no fear; in fact he felt prepared for battle. He had a sudden weird flashback of himself in a Civil War battle. He shook his head. *How strange*, he thought. The big biker, Axel, said, "Getting a little spooked, boy?"

Carl calmly said, "Actually, you are a little spooky, buddy. Why don't you and your girlfriend there-- pointing towards the smaller biker--just turn around and toddle back to your trikes and let us go on our way?"

Stepping closer and pointing his finger directly in Carl's face, Axel said, "The only way you are getting past me is after I wrap my arms around that gorgeous woman and squeeze those lovely ti. . ."

Before he could finish, Carl grabbed the biker's right hand and twisted his own body to the left, extending Axel's elbow and sending him screaming in pain directly into the lockers, face first.

Serenity was so shocked at how fast it happened, she laughed out loud. By then the other biker, Doodles, charged Carl like a wild pig. Once again Carl went through a very carefully choreographed move that allowed him to pull Doodles towards him and then over his extended foot, sending him directly into Axel. It was all very entertaining for Serenity so far. Carl appreciated his moves, but as the two angry men picked themselves up, Carl wondered what would happen next.

What happened was fast. As they charged him, more aware of his interesting ability and alacrity, they grabbed him by both arms and smashed his back into a brick hallway wall. Carl recoiled, grabbed Axel around the neck with his right arm, and kept twisting his body until they both hit the ground. This was no longer the delicate dance moves of Ti Chi. This was simply grappling and punching, something that the bikers had done many times, but Carl had never experienced. All he could do was use his considerable strength and ingenuity in trying to block their punches and dodge their knees and kicks. Serenity was frightened for Carl, as if they had been together for years (or much longer). He was seriously getting pummeled in a continued beating.

Carl was being slowly subdued, and put to the ground. Doodles was still standing and delivering kicks to Carl's legs as Carl tried to defend himself. He curled up, covering his head for a minute, but looked up and saw Axel with his arm wrapped around Serenity from behind with a grip on her right breast and his hand groping her legs. He stank of whiskey and loudly belched. Serenity thought she would throw up. Carl was mortified; he rolled over and popped up, grabbing the big guy by the neck with one hand and the groin with the other, charging. They both went down again, rolling on the ground. Carl grabbed Axel, punching him with his right fist and choking him with the other. He was fighting like a demon, but between the two adversaries, he was overpowered and suddenly pinned on the ground again.

Doodles threw himself on top of Carl, holding his arms down and pinning his body under his own sloppy bulk. There was blood under Carl's nose; he was weak and felt a searing pain in his kidney, where he had been jabbed at an angle. He couldn't see what happened to Axel, but he was afraid the thug was accosting Serenity again. He was simply too weak to get out from underneath Doodles. Then the looming shadow of Axel stood above them. Carl knew that this had gone beyond what he could handle. He closed his eyes and prayed, "*Om*, God, Guru, help me through this one, please! I finally found her."

All of a sudden the weight of Doodles seemed like it was being lifted off him. His arms were free, and he wiped the blood and sweat from his face with the sleeves on his forearms as he watched Doodles being levitated completely above him by some apparent supernatural force. He heard Serenity and another woman laughing and clapping as a huge figure of a man held the low-life biker aloft, turned him around, dropped him on his hands and knees, and kicked him in the butt.

"We have a saying for degenerates in Austin, Texas. Just get the hell out of here!"

And they did.

It was Abraham Finklestein aka "Brainiac." Angie and Abraham had been to the Red Onion, but when Carl didn't show on time, they came looking for him, thinking he'd still be at the class he'd mentioned. Next to meeting Serenity that night, Carl was never so glad to see any two people in his life. He was beat up and bruised but as cheerful as he could be. He hugged Angie and big Abe Finklestein. As they all walked toward the parking lot, Angie filled in the blanks for Serenity. They hit it off like long lost sisters.

After getting some water and beach towels out of the trunk of the Pontiac and cleaning himself up with Serenity's help, Carl said, "I'm hungry; let's go have a Mexican fiesta!"

As he started to get in his car, Serenity spoke up. "Wait just a minute, Carl; I need to get my puppy." She quickly skipped over to her VW and opened the door. A large silver and black puppy with ears that had just begun to stand up jumped out. He must have weighed 40 pounds. Serenity was very proud as she hooked a leather lead onto his collar and walked back to the group.

"This is my new puppy. . . No name yet; what should we call him?"

As if it had been planned for a hundred years or more, Abe, Angie, and Carl looked at each other, and without a cue, all said in unison, "Karma!"

Serenity clapped her hands in approval like a little kid, and smiled a blinding grin with her unforgettable dimples, creamy skin, clef chin, and perfect teeth. Carl's legs went weak, but you couldn't tell, he just looked happy beyond words. He suddenly gave Serenity the hug of a lifetime, and she kissed him an astoundingly passionate kiss. It was a long awaited reunion in more ways than any of them would ever know.

The following days and weeks were steeped in a multitude of climactic events for Serenity and Carl, uncanny epic flashbacks, and stories. The relationship was intellectually stimulating, totally satisfying physically and emotionally, but even more than any of the obvious worldly benefits, they both knew from the beginning that they were soul mates, linked spiritually since forever. And even though humans like a happy ending so much, Serenity and Carl knew that there would be no end to their divine love.

The most amazing aspect of Carl's soul evolution was Karma's impressions. Much like dogs have an incredible sense of smell and legendary hearing, they also have soul memories that are far more accurate than imaginable. Karma could remember his lives as a wolf reincarnated many times, until Kimo changed his karmic path, and Karma began to incarnate as a dog. As he exhibited classic unconditional love in the following years for

154

Serenity and Carl, he had clear flashbacks of countless events the three had experienced together. He acted by instinct and an indelible memory of everlasting love from his soul companions. It's no wonder that dogs' unconditional love is impervious to change. It's been there for countless eons.

Karma died on the day before Serenity and Carl had their first child. Their new friends and families, including Abe and Angie, were not surprised when they named their first son Karma Atman.

27122481R00086

Made in the USA
Lexington, KY
28 October 2013